7220

Lashawnda Woodard

Printed and Bound in the United States of America

Cover Design & Interior Layout: Jessica Tilles/TWA Solutions
First Printing: October 2020
978-0-578-76581-5

Dedication

My mom

Dell

My children: Booney, Tay, Toota, Tania

My grandchildren

FOREWORD

I am a young woman who has been through so much in my life. I know that I'm not the only one who has been through a few things, but so many of my challenges were self-inflicted. My mama was always there, raising us, making sure that all of our needs and a lot of our wants were met. But beyond making sure that we were cared for, Mama tried to make sure we learned the right lessons. She would talk and talk and talk about everything we were going to face in life. She did everything she could to prepare us for what was to come. My brothers and sisters and I had the teaching, it was up to us to decide what to do with it. My decision—like they say, my mother's words went in one of my ears and came out of the other. My mother tried to get me to listen, tried to get me to learn, tried to get me to make good choices. But what I did was listen and throw it away. It was as if I didn't want to learn because even with her teachings, I chose the wrong paths so many times.

But now, I have the benefit of hindsight. Looking back, I can see it all so clearly and there are so many things that I would change if I had the chance to go back and do it over. However, there's nothing I can do about what's behind me; I can only focus on the future.

I decided that there was something else that I could do as well. I decided that there was a way that I could pass on some of the lessons I learned to help someone else.

That's why I wanted to write this book. I wanted to share my story so that I could teach through the mistakes that I've made. I hoped to show someone that no matter your past, you can make it through. I wanted to share that no matter how down you may feel, if you can look up, you can get up. My prayer is that my story, my mistakes and my lessons will give someone else hope and the tools to turn around so that they can live their best life.

Chapter 1

As the seventh child of four boys and four girls, life was easy growing up at 7220 Halsted Street. The south side of Chicago, in the Englewood section of the city, was the place that I called home. My mother owned a three story flat building and we stayed on the second floor. Our apartment had three bedrooms; my mom had a bedroom, then there was one for the boys and the others were for the girls. Sometimes, it was crazy when four boys and four girls had to get up and get ready for school with just one bathroom, but we made it work. With relatives living below us, we were surrounded by a lot of family love and support.

My dad did come in and out of our lives, but he passed away in 1985, when I was only fourteen years old so I never really got to know him well. But it was funny, not having him in my life wasn't a big deal; I never cared about having a father.

I guess that was because I only knew my mother. For as long as I could remember, when it came to handling the family business, all of that was left up to my mother. She took care of everything. My mom had a lot on her plate making sure that eight children always had three meals a day and our lights and gas were always on. But it went beyond just making sure that we were fed. My mother took care of us in every way. Whether it was the holidays or our birthday, she handled it. Every Christmas, we had gifts. Every first day of school, we had the freshest clothes. All of our needs were met and a good amount of time, my mother was able to give us our desires, too, all on the income she earned cleaning at O'Hare, the Chicago airport before she got sick. My mom, even though she was the oldest mom out of all of my friends, was really a blessing. She was a strong woman who led by example and she tried her best to always get me to do the right thing.

Like I said, life was easy—except for one thing. If there was anything tough that my mother had to deal with, it was me...and the fact that I spent more time fighting in school than doing my schoolwork. When I was in grammar school, I fought all the time. I didn't fight because I enjoyed it, but because I really could fight. And because of my skills, there were kids in the school who used to egg me on. Everyone in the school loved to watch me fight because, well...I had those hands.

But while they loved it, my mother didn't. It was frustrating for her because I wouldn't stop. No matter what she said, no matter what she did, I kept on fighting. My mother had to spend hours up at the school having conferences with my teachers. After one of her long meetings with one of my teachers, my mom would come home upset and ask me, "Shawnda, why do you fight so much?"

I shrugged. "I don't know, Mama. People start with me and I just have to protect myself. I never start the fight."

That was the truth. Maybe it was because I was so skinny, quiet, and really kind of shy, that people thought they could get the best of me. But I was so underestimated. If anyone came for me, I went back at it with them, no matter what my mother said.

In the fifth grade, though my life changed. My new teacher, Mrs. McCoy was the first person who was ever able to get me to stop fighting and she did it by just treating me differently. From the first day when I met the petite forty-something-year-old black woman, I liked her. She may have been small, but she was feisty, the way I wanted to be when I got older. But the best thing about her was the way she talked to me. Every time she said something to me, I could tell that she believed in me.

"You're really smart, Shawnda," she said to me all the time. "I know you can do better."

Just those few words changed me. She helped me, encouraged me, motivated me and because of her, I wanted to do my best.

With that kind of positive attention, I focused on my school work and really did start doing better. I stopped fighting and settled down. It was the first time that I liked school.

But then, things changed. In the middle of the school year, the fifth grade was divided in two and I was transferred to a new class—Mr. White's class. He was a good enough teacher, I guess. He just wasn't interested in me the way Ms. McCoy had been. Instead of motivating me, he always compared me to my brother.

"You're Dell's sister, right?"

"Yeah."

"He was such a good student."

Having to follow in my brother's footsteps was really tough. It wasn't a compliment when the teacher mentioned his name and compared the two of us.

"Dell was so nice and not a trouble maker."

That always sounded like judgement to me and without the positive attention I had from Ms. McCoy, and feeling that Mr. White's comparisons were negative, rebellion began to rise up inside of me again. I lost my interest in school and that meant that I was fighting again, too. Things were so bad that by the end of the semester, I had to repeat the fifth grade.

Even for a ten-year-old this news of being left back was a tough thing to handle. Watching the kids who'd been in class with me advance to the sixth grade while I was still in the fifth grade, not only pissed me off, but embarrassed me so much. In reality, it made me feel like I was dumb.

Being left behind did something that my mother could never do—it made me change and buckle down so that I could focus on my school work. I stopped fighting, paid attention in class, and did what I was supposed to do because being left behind was something that was never going to happen to me again.

Having to repeat the fifth grade had long-lasting consequences. I was already quiet and shy, but being left back made me feel a little like being left out. When all of my friends were excited about going onto a new grade, I wasn't part of that. I felt so alone and I made sure nothing like that would happen to me again.

When I finally got to the sixth grade, things began to change a little when my social circle began to expand. It started with a friend I'd had from elementary school. I'd known Kris since about the second grade and from the moment I'd met her, she was so outgoing, bubbly, and personable, everyone liked her. All of our parents liked her, too, because she was polite and she was kind, just the kind of girl our parents wanted us to hang out with. So Kris had a lot of friends in school and all throughout the neighborhood.

When I was in the seventh grade, Kris brought me together with a couple of other girls: Michelle, Nessa, Tee and Sherice and we all started hanging out. Tee lived next door to me, so I knew her, but we became closer when we began hanging out with Kris. We were all the same age, but because I'd been left back, they were a year ahead of me. Nessa, was actually two years ahead of me and already in high school.

We began hanging out at Kris's house all the time. She had gotten us all together because Sherice had formed a dance group and wanted us to all be part of it. We all loved hip-hop, and back then, the thing was for girls to get together, form a group and have dance-offs at parties. At our first dance meeting, Sherice decided that the name of our group would be the Q Girls. It was her idea, her group, her name and we were all fine with it. We came up with routines and then, we'd go to parties and have dance offs with other groups.

Even though I was quiet and kind of shy, dancing was the thing that I truly loved, especially dancing with my girls. When I was dancing, I didn't feel shy at all. I felt free. I didn't feel as if I was being judged the way I was always judged in school.

But then when I went into the eighth grade, my friends all graduated, really leaving me behind this time when they went to high school. Once again, it felt as if I'd been left behind, but this time, I was physically alone, too. We still had the Q Girls, but now that Kris, Nessa and Tee were in a different school, they had new teachers, new friends, new classes, and even new conversations. They talked about things I knew nothing about.

Our friendship dynamics changed, too. Since Tee and I lived next door to each other, we used to walk over to Kris's house together all the time. But for some reason, she started leaving me behind and going over there by herself. I didn't know what happened but after she did that a few times, I just walked by myself.

We were still hanging out and definitely still dancing together, but that was when Kris and I became best friends. Nessa was still there, but since she was in the tenth grade, she had her own group of friends besides us.

Not only had I been left behind in classes, but I seemed to be slower than my girls in other ways, too. Once they got into high school, they talked about make-up and menstrual cycles, both topics that I didn't know much about. I was pretty much a tomboy and hated the thought of make-up all over my face. And I hadn't had my menstrual cycle yet, so I couldn't talk about that too much either.

What they loved to talk about the most, though, was something that I really couldn't talk about. Those girls loved to talk about boys. They talked about all the boys they liked, all the boys who liked them...and the boys they were having sex with! I couldn't believe they were having sex.

Sex became the topic of discussion so often, which I guess is the same for most teenage girls and boys, but it wasn't something that I was interested in. We still hung out together and we still danced together. All I could hope was that since this was my last year before I graduated, things would get better for me once I got to high school, too.

Chapter 2

September 6, 1986 changed my life forever. Finally! I was on my way to Paul Robeson High School. After waiting all of this time, I was very nervous. This was high school, that was a big deal and I knew that life was going to be different now.

I put on all the new clothes that I had for the first day, and even though I was excited that I would once again be in the same school as Kris and all the rest of my friends, I didn't go to school with them that morning. They all wanted to walk and I wasn't into that. The school was about a mile away, so I took the bus.

When I got there, though, I wasn't sure if I'd done the right thing. I needed my friends by my side because walking into that huge school was scary. First, the two-story building itself was much bigger than my elementary school and not only that, there were two buildings for the high school and the other building had four floors. I knew some of my classes would be in the building next door, and I couldn't imagine how I was going to find my way around.

The classrooms weren't my only problem. As I entered the building, I'd never seen so many students in one place before. There were kids everywhere. It felt a bit overwhelming because Guggenheim had been a small school with maybe about a hundred students or at least that's how it seemed to me. But now, there were several hundreds here and to be around this many people and not knowing any of them was really scary.

The building was big and there were lots of kids, but the worst part of high school was having to move around to all the different classes. Since the first grade, I'd been used to sitting in one classroom for the whole day, having one teacher teach every subject. Now, I had to go to different rooms for different subjects, nine different times. There were nine periods and that meant I had to find nine classrooms when I didn't even know where anything was...and one of my classes, biology, *was* in the other building. How was I supposed to handle all of this?

That first day was a serious struggle. The only thing that saved me was that I knew Kris and Nessa were close by or at least somewhere in this building and they would help me if I needed them. Of course, we didn't have any regular classes together since I was a freshman and they were all ahead of me. So for the whole first day I felt pretty alone, the new kid in a big school.

It was bad enough going from class to class, but the feeling of being alone really overwhelmed me during my lunch period. When I walked into the cafeteria, I had never seen a room so large; there had to be at least two hundred students in there. I looked around at all the kids talking to each other, laughing and playing like they'd all been friends for a long time. What was I supposed to do when I didn't know anyone?

After standing at the door for a couple of minutes, I just turned around and walked out, deciding to skip lunch completely. I was hungry, but I wasn't going to go back in there. I didn't have anywhere to go, though, so I walked around the building until one of the school security guards stopped me.

"Where are you supposed to be?" he asked me.

"I'm on my way to study hall," I lied.

He nodded. "You need to get there."

So I went to study hall and sat in the back of the class until the bell rang and I returned to my next class. Then, it was third period, my band class—and there was Kris.

"Hi," she said, jumping up when I came into the room.

I was so glad to see her. I hadn't planned to be in the band, but Kris was the one who told me to take the class. "We can play drums together," she said.

So that's what I did. I signed up and Kris and I were going to be on drums.

The moment I came into the band room, my very social and outgoing friend introduced me to everyone in the room. "This is my sister, Shawnda," she said.

"Hey Shawnda," they all said and I began to relax.

Because of Kris, I knew high school had just gotten a little bit easier for me. At least from now on, there would be a few faces that I would recognize.

❧

When I got home my mom was up and waiting for me. For the last few years, my mom hadn't been working. She was on public assistance because of her high blood pressure and often, that meant she spent a good part of the day in bed. But for my first day of high school, she was up and waiting to hear about my exciting day. "How was your first day in high school?"

I could hear in her voice that she really was happy for me and I didn't want to disappoint her, so I lied. "It was fun," I said, leaving out all the bad things about the school being too big and there being too many kids and me feeling lost. "I met a lot of people and it was good."

"Great. Do you have homework?"

I shook my head. "No."

"Okay, well you can go on outside. Just make sure that you're home by eight."

"Okay, Ma."

After I changed my clothes, I walked over to Kris's house, knowing that all the girls would be over there. I was right—they were all hanging out on the porch as if they'd been waiting for me.

Just like my mother, Kris asked, "How was your first day?"

We hadn't had the chance to talk about it in band and since I wasn't worried about them the way I was worried about my mother, I told my friends the truth. "It was too much," I said. "I don't like it." Then, I complained about everything that had gone wrong for me.

"It'll get better," they all told me.

"Yeah, you have us," Kris said. "You'll meet more people and you'll get used to the classes."

They all told me the same thing—how it would get easier and soon, I'd like high school.

"There's just one thing," Nessa said.

"What?"

She looked at the others and said, "The stairwell."

They all laughed and I frowned, not having any idea what they were talking about.

"There's this staircase," Nessa began to explain.

Apparently, there was a staircase in the building that led to nowhere and you didn't want to get caught going down there. If you did, everyone would know you were a freshman and make fun of you.

"It will be really bad if anyone sees you going down there," Nessa said. "You will get teased and it won't stop."

"Where is it?" I asked. "Where is the staircase?"

They tried to describe the staircase, but since I didn't know the building, I had no idea where they were telling me not to go.

All I could do was hope that I never found that staircase.

"Well, there's party on Lowe on Friday," Michelle said, changing the subject. "So, we're going," she told us as if we didn't have any other choice, but of course, we all wanted to go.

We hung out a bit more, talking about school and the fun we were going to have this year. Then, the conversation turned to the subject of boys like it always did and I still didn't say anything when they started talking about that. But today, it felt different as I sat around talking because now, I was in high school, too.

When it got close to eight o'clock, I left. It was time for me to head home and get ready for my second day of high school.

Chapter 3

The second day of school was just as scary as the first. Walking through the halls, I was still so surprised at how different high school was: the buildings, the classes and even all of those thick textbooks that I had for each class. That meant that I was going to have a lot of different homework assignments, too. I already didn't like school and now with all this extra work, I had a feeling that I was going to like school even less.

The only good thing was that I was making friends. Besides my girls, I made a new friend, Selina. I'd met her on the first day in English and then we had Biology together, too. From the moment I met Selina, she reminded me a lot of Kris. She was bubbly and outgoing and after she said hello, she talked to me as if we were already friends. Selina definitely made the next days in school so much better.

We sat in class and talked and laughed, making the teachers mad, I'm sure. But I couldn't help it. Selina was the only thing that got me through that first week. The work felt too advanced to me, so since I felt like I was lost anyway, I stopped paying attention in class. I already knew that I was in a lot of trouble.

There was one class that I did enjoy, though. Biology was good and I liked it for the same reason that I liked Ms. McCoy back in the fifth grade. My Biology teacher was just like Ms. McCoy—she challenged me to do the work.

But it wasn't enough to save me with the rest of my classes. For me, high school wasn't about classes or learning anything.

High school was just about being with my friends and going to parties.

❧

My friends were still into boys, and Kris had been hanging out with a guy she really liked. Anthony was older and already out of school, though he didn't graduate from high school; he had dropped out. But Kris was really into him.

She talked about him all the time until one day, she told me he was coming over to her house. "And I want you to be there when he comes."

"No," I told her. It was a school night and my mother had a strict curfew. I had to be home by eight. Plus, I didn't want to be at Kris's house with just her and Anthony and that's what I told her.

"It's not going to be just us. He's bringing his friend, Mark and I want you to meet him."

Now, I really told her no! Not only was I not having sex, but I didn't even know how to talk to boys; I didn't feel comfortable around them. Part of it had to do with me being shy, but another part of it was how I felt about myself.

I had really bad acne and growing up, that affected my self esteem so much because none of my friends were suffering from pimples all over their faces. I did everything I could to hide my face. Most of the time, I walked around with my head down, thinking that was the way to stop anyone from seeing my ugly face.

But while that was how I felt about myself, Kris didn't see me the same way. "Come on, Shawnda. You have to come to my house." And then, when she added, "I don't want to be there with them at my house by myself," I did what any best friend would do—I went to her house.

I was really nervous, though, but Chris made it comfortable for all of us. She introduced me to Anthony and his friend. Mark was a good-looking guy, dark complexion, about 5'10" and a nice smile that made me feel relaxed right away.

We started out just talking on the porch, which made me feel better. So by the time we went into her house, and Kris and Anthony went off to another room, leaving me alone with Mark in the living room, I felt fine. I knew he wasn't going to try anything with me.

Mark kept the conversation easy by asking me a lot of questions:

"So, how old are you, Shawnda?"

"Fourteen."

"What school do you go to?"

"I'm at Paul Robeson," I said. "Are you in high school?" I asked him.

He chuckled. "Nah."

I knew he was older, but I just had a feeling that he was like Anthony and he hadn't finished high school.

He asked, "Do you have a boyfriend?"

"No." I shook my head, wondering why he'd asked me that.

He grinned. "Good. Keep it that way."

That made me frown. "Why would you say that?"

"Just keep it that way until you finish school because boys are no good. Boys only want one thing—sex."

He was talking to me like a big brother and I really appreciated that. We just kept talking until about an hour later, Kris and Anthony came out from the bedroom.

"Let's go for a ride," Kris said.

I was up for that. Anthony and Mark had driven up in a really cool car and I wanted to go for a ride. Kris and Anthony got in the back of the car and I sat upfront with Mark as we just drove around the neighborhood and listened to music. Mark kept talking to me, asking me questions. Again, I felt like I was talking to one of my big brothers and I could tell Mark wanted to just be my friend. He cared about me.

We'd been driving around for a while when I glanced at my watch. I had forgotten all about the time. It was a little after eight and we weren't anywhere near my house. I moaned; I was going to be in such trouble. "I have to get home," I told Mark.

"Okay," he said as he turned the car around. "We'll head back now."

It still took us about fifteen minutes to get to my house and now, I was really late. I might have gotten away with it—except when Mark pulled up in front of the house, my sister, Mia was sitting on the porch.

This was going to be a problem because if there was one thing my mom didn't play with, it was curfew. Not only was I late, I was late because Kris and I were hanging out with these two guys.

Before I got out of the car, I saw my sister watching me and when she turned around and walked into the house, I knew what was going to happen. When I got up to our second floor apartment, my mother was already calling me. By the time she finished yelling at me for missing my curfew, I was on punishment.

"For a week," my mother said. "No phone calls, no being outside. Just go to school and then come home."

I couldn't believe it. Just because I'd been helping Kris out. The next day after school I came straight home and when I didn't show up at her house, Kris came over to mine.

"Where have you been?" Kris asked me when I came out onto the porch.

I wasn't supposed to have any company, but my mother loved Kris. She was like one of her kids, so she didn't count when I was on punishment, which was good. At least I could talk to her and tell her that I was mad at her.

"Oh, my God," I said. "I'm in trouble because of you. I'm on punishment."

She looked like she was confused. "On punishment? Why? What did you do?" she asked as if she didn't remember that I was with her!

"I stayed out too late last night and it was a school night. You know how my mom is about that."

Kris shook her head as if she couldn't believe it. These kind of strict rules were hard for Kris to understand because her mother was a little less strict, which was why we always hung out at her house.

"Okay, well," Kris began as if my punishment wasn't a big deal. "I wanted to ask you about Mark. Did you like him?"

I shrugged. "Yeah, he was cool."

"Did y'all fuck?"

"No!" I said. "When would I have done that?" I couldn't believe she asked me that. Kris knew I was a virgin and if she really knew me as a friend, she knew I was going to stay that way. "And he didn't try anything either," I said. "He talked to me like he was my big brother."

"Dang. Oh well, I'm gonna find you someone."

"Kris, I don't want a boyfriend. I'm just fourteen. I'm cool."

But that wasn't good enough for my friend. I could tell by the look in her eyes that she was determined to help me find a boyfriend, so that I could have one just like her.

Chapter 4

I was glad to be off punishment by that weekend so that I could go to that party over on Lowe that Michelle had told us about. My friends went to way more parties than I did, but now that I was in high school, I wanted to hang out like they did.

Together, we all walked the four blocks to the part together, excited about going to the house party. But when we walked up to the house where there were all these kids hanging out, Kris said, "Oh my God. This is Anthony's house."

I frowned. "He didn't tell you he was having a party?"

She shook her head. "No."

I thought that was strange; he was her boyfriend. But we all walked inside anyway, and went down to the basement that was packed with teenagers. There were kids from our neighborhood, kids from our school, and lots of kids that we didn't know.

Anthony and Mark were both over at the DJ table and they weren't alone. There were all of these girls, some of them older, hanging all over both of them. That didn't bother me; Mark wasn't my boyfriend, but I wondered if it bothered Kris because I knew she really liked Anthony and they'd been having sex. But even though he looked at her and didn't say anything, she seemed fine. I knew she wasn't one hundred percent good with it, but she left it alone.

Anthony didn't speak to Kris, but Mark came over and spoke to us.

"Hey, how you doin'?" Mark asked me.

"I'm cool. I didn't know this was your party."

"Yeah. Just chill and have a good time."

"Okay," I said.

"But don't stay out too late," he teased.

I just laughed with him, but I didn't want to be on punishment again. And with all of the smoking and drinking that was going on in this party, if my mother found out about this, I would be on permanent punishment if she didn't kill me.

But I wasn't thinking about my mother because we were having a good time. We partied to all kinds of house music, LL Cool J, Public Enemy and Eazy E. We drank a little, though we didn't smoke. We just danced and hung out. I wasn't paying any attention to the time, so when the party was over and I saw it was 12:30, I was shocked. I didn't have to be home until 11:00 on the weekends, but I was still really late. I was going to be in trouble once again, but at least I'd had a good time.

It didn't take us long to walk home, but this time was different. No one was on the porch waiting for me. I was able to sneak into the house, get up the stairs and into my bed without anyone realizing that I was an hour and a half late coming home from the party.

I wasn't going to be in trouble after all.

While I enjoyed the parties and my friends, I still wasn't feeling high school. My only saving grace were Fridays. I lived for Fridays because school was over and that's when all the parties happened. Before I could go out, though, I had to go to church first. Not church services, but choir practice. My sister, Vita, with her no-singing ass, and I were in the choir. It didn't matter that she couldn't sing. We weren't at one of those big churches where you had to try out to sing on Sundays. We were in a much smaller church where whoever wanted to be in the choir could be and my mother wanted me and my sister in the choir.

So on Fridays, right after school, we went to choir practice. That only lasted about an hour or so, and then, it was time for the parties. My only challenge was that even though I was in high school, I couldn't get my mother to change my 11:00 curfew. That wasn't fair to me because my friends could stay out later. I wasn't even sure of Kris's curfew.

But my mother wasn't going to change it, so if I wanted to go to the parties, I had to follow her rules. I went to all the Friday night parties and always had a blast, even though the parties were all the same. The house would be packed, kids were smoking, drinking, dancing, just having a good time. I never danced at any of the parties unless the Q Girls were having a dance off. That was the only time that I would dance in front of a lot of people.

At most of these parties, it was nothing but fun. No fights broke out and at the end, we'd walk home together. Almost every Friday, I had to sneak in because I was always late, but I was lucky that no one was waiting up for me

Then, on Saturdays, we'd all go over to Kris's house and chill out there. Every weekend it was just about the same thing every Friday and Saturday—and I loved it.

One Saturday, though, when we were hanging out at Kris's house, Nessa told us that there was a party that night.

"Where?" the rest of us asked her.

"The China Dolls are having a party on Aberdeen, and Tony is the DJ."

The China Dolls and Tony? That was going to be a great party. The China Dolls were another dance group from a different school and Tony was Nessa's cousin. We all knew this was going to be the party to be at. We were all excited.

"Okay, let's go get ready for the party," Kris said.

Before I could do that, I had to ask my mom. Kris's mom was going to let her go, so I was the one who wasn't sure. It was going to take a lot since I'd been at a party last night and I knew my mother didn't like me going to all of these parties. But when I got home and saw my mom in the kitchen, I pulled up the nerve to ask her if I could go.

"Ma, there's a party tonight. Can I go with Kris and the rest of my friends?"

When she looked at me like I was crazy, I already knew the answer. "You went to a party last night," she said just like I expected her to say. "I'm not going to be having all of this partying going on around here."

I felt so bad by the time I got to my bedroom. My friends were going to go and have such a good time. But then, when I thought about what my mother had said, I realized that she hadn't said no. All she'd said was that she wasn't going to have all of this partying going on. That meant that I still had a chance and I called my secret weapon—Kris.

When she answered the phone, I told her that she had to call my mom if she wanted me to go to the party.

"Okay," she said.

I knew that would do it. Like everyone else, my mother loved Kris. I didn't know what she was going to say to my mom, but I knew it would work. I was right. My mom told me that I could go to the party!

I was so excited, but I didn't have much time to get dressed. I had my clothes ready, though—my Guess jeans, of course and a cute top. Like we always did, we met at Kris's before we walked over to Aberdeen. Like all the other parties, this one was packed, too. Only this time, we had to pay to get in. That cost a dollar and then, we could buy sodas inside for fifty-cents. They were making money at this party.

We'd been there for about an hour, when someone shouted out, "China Dolls!" And then a bunch of people joined in, yelling, "China Dolls! China Dolls! China Dolls!"

After a couple of seconds, we started shouting, "Q Girls, Q Girls, Q Girls!"

It escalated, and only one of two things was going to happen—either we were going to have a dance off or we were going to fight. I was ready for either one. But I didn't have to do anything because Michelle jumped into the middle of the floor and started dancing. So the China Dolls had one of their girls dance against Michelle, and the chanting continued.

We shouted until we were all sweaty, we shouted until we were all tired. But we never stopped. We couldn't stop until the music stopped. When the DJ stopped the music, it was clear that Michelle was the winner by all of the cheers that filled the basement for her.

Then, the party spilled outside, I thought it was fight time. Usually, that was the only reason people went outside and I was always ready to fight. But it seemed as if I was the only one in my group who wanted to fight—well, except for Sherice. We'd just met, but she was just like me. She was down for the battle.

But Michelle and Tee didn't want to fight at at all. After that, no one wanted to party anymore and we walked home. I was mad. I thought I knew the Q Girls, but I guess I didn't. They were all mouth, but scary asses. Why didn't they want to fight?

On the walk home, no one said anything. They all knew I was mad, they all knew how much I liked to fight. But it was cool. I got over it. Those girls were always going to be my friends. At least, that's what I thought.

Chapter 5

One thing about Sundays—no matter what I did on Saturday, I had to get up and go to church the next day. Even though I was so tired from the China Dolls party last night, it didn't matter. My mother had told all of us a long time ago that until we turned eighteen, we were going to church every Sunday unless we were sick. There was only one way for us to get a pass. We had to be so sick that we were throwing up, had a fever, and couldn't get out of bed. That was the only time; every other Sunday, our butts were going to be in church.

But even though I had to drag myself to church, the good thing was that after the services, we never did anything. My mother said that Sunday was God's day and it was a day of rest. We couldn't even wash or iron our clothes for the week on Sundays. Either we took care of that on Saturday, or we got up extra early on Monday morning. The only thing we could do was eat and watch television. After that party last night, I was glad for my mother's Sunday rules.

On Monday, it was back to school and I met up with Selina at the corner for what had become our normal walk together for the last couple of months. I had stopped taking the bus, and started walking with my friends and Selina joined us. She and I were becoming good friends because we were both freshman.

As we were walking, some of the kids walking behind us started talking about the Pep Rally that was coming up soon and everyone was pretty excited about that. I had no idea what they were talking about, so I asked Kris.

"Oh, that's when everyone in the school gets together before the games. All the freshmen, sophomores, juniors and seniors sit together with their class and everyone cheers along with the cheerleaders as the basketball and football teams are introduced. Oh, and the band plays, too. It really is a lot of fun with everyone screaming and acting crazy. Pep rallies are supposed build school spirit."

"So when is the rally?"

"It's going to be Friday afternoon during school." By that time, we were at school and Kris had to rush off to class. "Okay, I'll see you later in band," she said.

"Okay," I said, knowing I wasn't going to see her. Like so many of my other classes, I had stopped going to band weeks before.

When Kris left us alone, Selina said, "I have band third period, but I never go."

"I don't go anymore either," I said. And we laughed about it.

I'd been in high school for about one month and I'd started cutting classes because I just didn't like school. Like I said, the work was too advanced for me and when I tried to pay attention, I felt so lost. I felt better when I skipped class. That didn't make me feel dumb, but all that did was put me further behind. As the weeks in school passed, it was getting worse. I was doing it to myself by missing so many classes, but I didn't know what to do or how to fix it.

Selina was just like me and so many times, we skipped class together. We did go to English, though, because we had a lot of fun in Ms. Moore's class. That was where we met up with Renee, another freshman who was loud and funny and the three of us sat together and just clowned the whole time. That didn't make Ms. Moore happy, but I was more focused on having fun than doing my work.

My next class was Geometry and that was actually a class that I sometime enjoyed because I understood what Ms. Perkins was teaching. But then, Selina and I would skip third period, wandering the halls until one of the security guards caught up with us and made us go to study hall. It was funny; I had never heard of study hall before I got to high school, but Selina and I missed so many classes, we became study hall queens until they started checking IDs.

Over the weeks, our days pretty much continued the same way. Some classes we went to, some we didn't. The best part of the school day was at the end for me. I would mostly walk home with Selina and Kris and we would just take our time, talking and laughing. One day, though, when we were about two blocks from the school, Anthony and Mark rolled up next to us in their car.

"Hey, what's going on?" Anthony asked us.

We stopped walking to talk to them.

"Do you want a ride home?" Anthony asked.

Before Selina and I could say anything, Kris hopped in the car. So Selina and I got in, too. I introduced Selina to Anthony and Mark, but all of Kris's attention was already on Anthony. They hadn't been hanging out much together after that party he gave with Mark, but I guessed Kris was okay with that now.

When they dropped us off at Kris's house, Selina and I got out and I walked home from there. Getting home from school was one of the best parts of the day for me—it was time to eat. Every day, I'd walk into the house wondering what my mom was cooking. Every day, I said the same thing, "That smells good; I'm starving."

"Stop saying that," my mom said the way she always did. "You're not starving. There are people who are really starving in this world. You're just hungry."

"Yes," I said.

"And why are you so hungry? Didn't you eat lunch at school?"

"Yes, I'm just hungry."

"Well, after you eat dinner, make sure you wash the dishes," she said, because that was my chores for this week. "And no going out today," she added.

Oh man! I hated the days when my mother wouldn't let me me go out. I wanted to ask her why I had to stay in the house, but even if I asked, she never gave me a good answer. She would just say, "'Cause I said so," so I didn't even bother to ask her today.

After dinner and after my chores, my sister, Mia and I just sat on the porch.

"So, how's high school?"

I told her what I told everyone when they asked that question. "It's okay," I told her.

"Have you met any new people?"

That was the best part of high school for me—my friends. "Yeah," I said. "I'm friends with this girl named Selina. She's a freshman, too. And there are a couple of other girls I've met."

"What about boys?" She grinned. "Have you met any boys?"

"No!" I said and we laughed.

"That time will come sooner or later," she told me. "Don't rush it, just stay focused on school." Her words sounded a lot like what Mark had told me.

My siblings and I were close and I was grateful because I knew there were a lot of brothers and sisters who didn't get along at all. Yeah, my brothers, sisters and I had the normal sibling squabbles over the TV and who had to do what chores. But we really loved one another, we supported each other, and I knew I was lucky to have them. No matter what I was going through in my life, I never wanted to forget that how important they all were to me.

There were some days when I walked to school and then other days when I took the bus. The next morning, Kris called and asked me not to take the bus and just walk to school with her because there was something that she wanted to talk about.

I was pretty sure she wanted to talk about what happened with Anthony yesterday, so once I met her at her house and we started walked, I asked Kris, "So what happened with Anthony?

"We went to his house and we had sex."

"Really? After he hasn't been talking to you?"

"I know, but I'm so in love with him."

When I said, "Really?" again, she told me she was joking.

"I don't really love him, but I like him a lot."

After a couple of moments of quiet, I asked her, "So, how was it? Having sex?"

"It was cool," she said. Then after a pause, she said, "You still haven't had sex, huh?"

I shook my head. "No."

"Why not?"

"I'm not ready yet."

"Everyone is having sex. You're the only virgin I know," she said.

We laughed together after she said that, but by the time we got to school, Kris had me thinking about what she'd said. Was I really the only virgin left? I couldn't have been.

In class, I couldn't wait to meet up with Selina. Before the class began, I asked her, "Are you a virgin?"

"No," she said as if she couldn't believe I would ask her that. "I'm not a virgin." Then, she went on to tell me about her boyfriend, Herman, from her church. But after she told me about him, she looked at me sideways. "Are you a virgin?"

I nodded. "Yeah," I said.

I didn't expect what she did next—she laughed. She laughed so hard that she made me laugh. We laughed for so long, it was like we were cracking up for no reason.

Finally she said, "Okay, we're going to have to find you somebody to have sex with. You cannot be a virgin."

"Nope." I shook my head. "No thanks, you don't have to find me anybody." I was good being a virgin and I didn't know why I couldn't get anyone to understand that.

Selina and I made our way to Biology, but when we got there, I got the surprise of my life.

Mrs. Crowder said, "Before you leave class today, I'll be giving you your grades for the first semester, so if you didn't get all of your assignments and homework in, it's too late.

I was confused. First semester? It was over already. I sat in that class feeling a little scared. I didn't have to see my grade in Biology or in any of the other classes to know that I had fucked up. My mother was gonna kick my ass when I brought home these failing grades.

Standing up, I said to Mrs. Crowder, "I'll give you three hundred dollars if you give me an A." Everyone in the class laughed and I did, too, but I was only half-kidding. I mean, I didn't have three hundred dollars, but I was willing to do anything to get a good grade, rather than go home and face my mother.

She glared at me. "Sit down. You haven't done anything in my class this semester."

I sat down, but for the rest of the class, I was worried. When class ended, Selina said, "Girl, these grades...I know I'm in trouble."

"Me, too. We have to start going to class and doing our work."

Selina shook her head. "It's too late now."

"Well, it may be too late for this semester, but we can get on the right track for next semester. We have to start fresh."

We both agreed and promised that we would do much better. But I was going to have to talk to my mother about this. The best thing for me was to handle it now.

❧

It was going to take me some time to figure out how to talk to my mother and to find the best time to do it. I decided that I wanted to get it over with so when I got home, after I finished my choirs (this week, it was cleaning the bathroom), and dinner, and hanging out a little while watching videos, I got up enough nerve to go to my mother's bedroom.

"Ma, can I talk to you about something?"

"Sure," she said. "But I have to go to the store, so walk with me."

Going to the store might be even better, I thought. While we were walking, I could just tell her that my grades weren't going to be good. Maybe she would go easier on me if we were outside rather than in the house.

But before I could say anything, my mother brought up what I wanted to talk to her about. We had only walked about a block when she said, "I got a call from your teacher, Mrs. Crowder today."

Inside, I said: Wow! Was she kidding me? Aloud, I said, "What did she say?" even though I kind of already knew.

My mother said, "She told me that you tried to bribe her to get an A."

I couldn't believe my teacher called my mother to tell her that. Didn't she know I was kidding? I was only fifteen, I didn't have three hundred dollars.

She continued, "And she said that you haven't been doing your homework or your class assignments. She said she was giving you an F. So you know there's no more going outside for a week."

This was bad. If I got that kind of punishment for one F in one class, what would I get when I told my mother the truth about all of my grades. For a moment, I didn't want to tell her, but since we were talking about it, I knew this would be the best time to just get it over with. "Ma, I failed all my classes."

She stopped walking for a moment and she just looked at me as if she couldn't believe what I was saying.

"I didn't know grades came out so soon," I explained. "Or I would have worked to get them better before they came out."

"It doesn't matter when grades come out, Shawnda," she said. "You're supposed to be doing your assignments and your homework all along. So now, you got all F's?" She sounded so disappointed. "Well that means no going outside, no company, no phone calls, no anything until you bring your grades up."

I said, "Does that mean no church on Sunday either?"

I was trying to make a joke to make her and myself feel better, but my mother didn't crack a smile. "Be funny if you want to and I can make your punishment longer."

Well that joke didn't go over too well. But at least I got it over with and now my mother knew. That was that and I was grounded. I was just going to have to do better the next time.

Chapter 6

On my way to school the next day, when I got to the corner where I always met up with Selina, she wasn't there. But on the way, I saw Renee, but not Selina.

"Have you seen Selina?" I asked her.

"Yeah, she went to school early because she got grounded. Her grades were really bad."

"The same thing happened to me," I told Renee.

"Really? Mine weren't that bad, but they weren't good either. I'm going to have to bring my grades up."

"Me too, if I ever want to go out again."

At school, I found out that all of my friends had received good grades, too. I knew for sure that I had to get it together, especially when Nessa started talking about the party that was coming up on Friday.

I was so mad when I told them, "I won't be able to go to the party."

"Why not?" Kris asked me.

"My report card. I got all F's."

My friends looked at me the way my mom had. They couldn't believe it and now, I was a little embarrassed.

Sherice told me, "Don't worry. You have time to bring your grades up. Second and fourth semesters are when the credits come out. You need five credits to pass to be a sophomore. So you have time to get those credits. But you want to get your credits because if you don't, you'll be a demo."

They all moaned when she said that and I frowned. "What's a demo?"

"That's a sophomore taking freshman classes all over again."

Oh, my God. That sounded like what happened to me in the fifth grade when I was left back. I certainly didn't want that to happen to me again.

Then, it got worse—the girls started talking about homecoming in a couple of weeks. "You don't want to miss that," she told me.

No, I didn't. I didn't want to miss my first homecoming in high school. Everyone talked about how much fun that was between the games and the parties and all the people who had graduated from Robeson over the years coming back to the school. I was going to fix this. I had to.

That afternoon in between classes, I finally saw Kris who was the only one I hadn't seen this morning. She was in the hallway talking to this really big, kinda fat guy. I'd seen her talking to him a couple of times before, but I didn't know who he was. This time, I walked right up to them and waited for them to stop talking. When he walked away from her, I asked, "Who is that guy?"

"That's Moore. He's on the football team."

"Really?"

"Yeah, he's really nice and I kinda like him."

"You like him? I thought you liked Anthony."

She shrugged. "I still like him a lot, but he has a lot of girlfriends and I'm not stupid; he's not serious about me. But he is having another party next week, I heard."

"Are you going?" I asked her.

"Yeah, of course. Even if he's hanging out with other girls, he gives a good party. What about you?"

I shook my head. "I'm out sure. I'll have to convince my mom because right now, I'm grounded because of my grades."

"Why? What did you get?"

"All F's," I told her.

Her reaction was like everyone else's. Her eyes were wide when she said, "For real?" She didn't give me a chance to respond to her. She said, "All you have to do is go to class and do your work, Shawnda. It's not that hard. You can still pass for the whole semester."

"That's what Nessa and Sherice said this morning."

"Yeah, you don't want to be a demo."

Everybody was telling me the same shit, but although I was going to try, I knew it wasn't going to be easy for me. How was I going to focus on my classes when I hated school so much? I hated school with a passion.

Kris said, "Well, I'll see you after school, okay?" as she rushed off to her class.

I told her I'd see her later, but then, I took my time getting to my class when the school bell rang. Damn, now I was late. Trying to do better wasn't getting off to a good start. When I got to my English class, I opened the door, and asked Ms. Moore if I could still come into the class even though I was late.

She looked me up and down. "You got a quarter?"

"Yes," I told her and she nodded, letting me in.

When I took my seat next to Selina, she cracked up, laughing. "You gotta pay to come into class?"

Then, Ms. Moore came after me again. "Where's your notebook and pen?" she asked me.

I shrugged. I was so unprepared. I never packed my school books because I never opened them anyway. "I don't have anything," I said.

Selina spoke up. "I'll give her paper and a pen, Ms. Moore."

The teacher nodded and then, I got to work. Selina, Renee and I were quiet in the class for the first time since we'd all met.

We were all serious about doing better in class, but I wasn't sure this was going to help me. I still hated sitting in there, trying to listen to the teacher.

Once the class was over, Selina said, "Come with me."

"Where?"

"I have some stuff in my locker," she said. "I can give you a notebook and a pen for the rest of your classes. You said you wanted to do better right?" I nodded. She said, "Well, you have to have a notebook and pen for the rest of your classes."

I followed her to the locker room on the second floor and I was shocked. I didn't even know this locker room existed. She gave me the pen and paper and then asked, "So how long are you on punishment?"

"My mom said until I bring my grades up, but knowing her, it will be just for a week," I said.

"Me, too." She shook her head and we started laughing. "We've got to do better."

I said, "I know. We'll be missing out on all the fun this weekend."

"We just have to make sure this doesn't happen again," she said, as we made our way to Geometry class.

Once I got to the classroom, Mrs. Perkins raised her eyebrows when she saw me. "Where have you been?"

"I've been sick," I said.

She nodded. "Okay, just bring a doctor's note with you next time so your absences won't be held against you." I told her okay, surprised that she really believed me. But then she said, "It's hard to be somebody, and easy to be a nobody."

Damn! That sounded like something that my mom would say to me. I got the message and sat down, and tried to stay focused on the class.

After Geometry, I saw Kris and Moore in the hallway again. Damn, they were spending a lot of time together. This time, though, Kris introduced us. "This is my sister, Shawnda and Shawnda, this is Moore. He's on the football team," she repeated what she'd told me this morning.

"Oh man," I said. "That's good."

"Yeah, y'all have to come to one of our games."

"Sure, no problem." We talked and joked and laughed a little. Moore was loud and I liked him.

When he finally walked off leaving me and Kris alone, I asked her, "Is he your boyfriend now?"

"Be for real. We're just talking. But I told you, he's really nice and I like him."

"He seems nice." But then, I cut off our conversation because I didn't want to be late for Biology. I really was going to try to do better, so I told Kris I'd see her after school, and then I caught up with Selina who was heading to Biology, too.

"We're gonna have to walk a little and run a little to make it to class on time," she said.

We did make it to class, right before Mrs. Crowder closed the door. But once we sat down, I had another problem. I had to share Selina's book.

Mrs. Crowder saw me sitting close to Selina and she frowned. "Where's your book, Shawnda?"

I was still mad at her for calling my mother, so I said, "The dog ate it."

That made everyone in the class—except Mrs. Crowder—crack up. The teacher didn't crack a smile.

Mrs. Crowder said, "If you lost that book, you're going to have to pay for it."

I wanted to tell her to just leave me alone and teach the class.

At least I was here and trying to do better, but she was making it harder for me. She did go back to teaching the class, but it wasn't good for me. I didn't understand any of the shit she was teaching; I was so lost. It was the longest forty-five minutes of my life.

But in order for me to bring my grades up, I had to make up the work and I needed Mrs. Crowder's help to do that. At the end of the class, I asked her what I could do to improve my grade. She gave me make-up homework for extra credit.

I made it through the rest of that day, but it was the longest day of the school year—going to every class, trying to pay attention when I didn't know what most of the teachers were talking about. How in the world would I be able to catch up?

Now I understood what my mother meant by doing all of my work in the beginning and continuing to do it all along. I would have been fine, but now, I didn't know shit and it seemed impossible that I was going to be able to fix this.

❧

Friday was the day of the pep rally and I was so ready to see what all the hype was about since everybody had been talking about this all week. That morning, I met up with Selina and she told me that she had been doing better with her assignments and homework all week. "I know my grades are going to go up. Thank God. What about you?" she asked me.

I shook my head. "It's hard catching up," I told her.

"Yeah, I know. But I've been working very hard. And you can do it, too."

As we headed toward our classroom, we suddenly heard, "Shawnda, Selina!"

Turning around, we saw loud-ass Renee, waving. Since we were all heading to the same class, we waited for her.

When she caught up with us, Renee said, "Are y'all ready for the test today?"

I frowned. "Wait, what test?"

Renee looked at me. "Our English quiz."

"Shit. No." How had I missed that? A test? Damn, I wasn't paying attention to anything.

"Well don't get upset. Just read a couple of pages when we get into class," Selina said. "And then, I'll try to help as much as I can."

That sounded like a plan, but when we got into the classroom, Mrs. Moore had other plans for me. She had to shake things up a bit.

"You sit up from, Shawnda," she said pointing to a chair right in front of her desk. "So that I can see you." She even separated Selina and Renee as if she knew what we were up to.

I didn't even get mad. How could I? She was a smart lady. So I just sat where she told me to and then I did the best I could on the quiz. At this point, all I wanted to do was make it through this class and the next one, so that I could get to the pep rally.

After two more periods, Selina, Renee and I finally walked over to the gym. When we got there, I was shocked. It was the first time I'd been in there when it was packed like this. Every inch of the bleachers was filled with students. We made our way to the freshman section and right away, we got into the excitement and energy of the rally.

"Where my freshman at?" the cheerleaders shouted.

And our section screamed. Then, they did the sophomores, juniors, and seniors and each class tried to out-yell the other. It was so loud in there it felt like the walls were vibrating, even before the band came out. Then, the football and basketball teams were introduced, along with the coaches. I hadn't ever cheered and laughed and had so much fun.

At the end of the rally, the crowd spilled out into the hallways and all of that cheering and laughter and noise just continued. All of the teachers and security guards were shouting, trying to get us to calm down and go to the next class.

I didn't even know we had to go back to class. I thought after the pep rally they would let us go home since the big game was tonight. Like all the other kids, I finally made my way to my next class, but even in there, I could feel the excitement. At the end of the day, I caught up with my girls.

They were still excited from the pep rally. "Are you going to the game?" Kris asked me.

I was pretty sure she remembered that I was on punishment, but I told them I couldn't go. "I won't be off punishment till Monday."

"Oh," she said. "Well, remember to buy a ticket anyway to support the team.

I was wondering why would I do that? They participated in all the school activities, but at this point, all I wanted to do was play catch up.

Since they were all going to the game, I got ready to walk home alone. But as I was leaving the school, I saw Nessa. "Hey, you're not going to the game," I asked since it looked like she was headed out the door, too.

"Nope," she said. "I'm heading home."

So we walked together, something we hadn't done in a while. We started talking and of course, began speaking about our grades. I told her my grades were the reason why I couldn't go to the game tonight.

"My grades aren't where I want them to be either," Nessa said, "but I want to do everything I can because I just want to graduate on time. I'm so ready to move out and get my own place."

Wow, I wasn't even thinking about something like that. At least she had a reason to want to do better. For me, I couldn't find one. Everyone was trying to do better, but I just didn't care.For the rest of the walk home, we talked about the boys in school, but my thoughts remained on how I just didn't like being at Paul Robeson High School.

At home, while my mother cooked dinner, I told her about the pep rally. It was the only thing that had been exciting for me at school. "It was really fun," I told her.

"High school is supposed to be fun," she said. "Going to games and cheering for your teams. It's not about partying all the time. There's a lot more to life." Then, she asked me something that she'd never asked me before, "What do you want to be when you grow up?"

I shrugged. "I don't know."

"Well, it's time for you to start thinking about that. You're in high school now and you're getting older, Shawnda. You're going to be surprised how fast time will go by."

"Okay, Ma, I'll think about it."

"You're focusing in school, right?"

"Yes," I lied.

"You're not into some little boy, are you?"

"No!"

She nodded. "Okay. School first, boys later. Don't no man want a woman who's not doing nothin' for themselves. You want to get a good education so you can get a nice job and live independently."

"Okay, Ma," I said again.

Then, after staring at me some more, my mom said, "Listen, if you find yourself getting involved with some little boy, make sure you get some birth control. You don't want to get pregnant.

You want to finish high school so that you can do something with your life."

"Okay," and then without taking a breath, I said, "Can I go outside today?"

She shook her head. "You ain't heard nothing I said, have you?"

"I hear you."

She sighed before she said, "Yeah, go on out, but have your ass back in this house by nine."

"Ma, it's Friday."

"I don't care if it's Tuesday. Be back by nine o'clock. Take it or leave it."

So of course, I took it because it meant that I was no longer on punishment. And I used that time to walk over to Kris's house. When I got there, my friend was shocked to see me. "Your mother let you out?"

"Yeah," I told her.

"So you're going to the party?"

"No. I have to be back at nine, so there's no way I can go. What time are y'all leaving?"

"I don't even know," Kris said. "None of the other girls are going."

"What?"

"Yeah. So if I can find someone to go with, then, I'll go. I want to see Anthony."

Kris's mother pushed open the screen door and stepped out onto the porch. After she said hi to me, she told Kris, "You're not going to any party tonight. All you want to do is party, party, party. Well, not today! You're going to stay home tonight."

At first, I was shocked. This was the first time I'd ever heard Kris's mom tell her that she couldn't go somewhere. When her mom went back into the house, I started cracking up. I guessed Kris's situation wasn't that much different from mine.

"Well, this is going to be boring," Kris said, pouting a little. "What are we going to do all weekend?"

"I don't know." I shrugged. "Maybe we can go to see a movie."

For the rest of that night, though, we didn't do anything except sit on that damn porch until 8:30 and then, I walked my ass home so that I wouldn't make my mom mad. I'd just gotten off punishment and I didn't want her to even think about putting me back on.

Chapter 7

Nothing was more boring that having nothing to do on a Saturday. But then, Kris called me and asked if I could come out.

"Yeah," I said.

"Okay, good. We're going over to 63rd Street to steal some pants for the party tonight."

"That's cool. Meet me on Halsted," I told her. "That way, we can just hop on the bus."

Just a half hour later, I caught up with Kris, Sherice and Nessa's cousin, Coco, and we headed over to the stores on 63rd Street. We'd done this before and our plan was easy enough. We went into the store, tried on some pants and then if we liked them, we put our pants right on top of them. Even though we got away with it, we didn't do this too often. It wasn't like we had to steal clothes. All of our mothers took care of us pretty well, but sometimes, we just wanted to get something new.

After an hour, we headed back home and when I asked my mother if I could go to the party that night, I was so excited when she said yes. That night, we rolled into the party together: me, Kris, Michelle, Tee, Nessa and Sherice and all of us were wearing our new clothes. Like all the other parties, when we got there, the house was packed with kids. But the thing that stood out the most to us were the China Dolls.

They were there looking really cute. All of them were in matching shirts and pants and looked real good. But the party was fire like they always were. The only thing was that it ended earlier than normal after a fight broke out. We left, and on the walk home, we talked about the party, but especially about the China Dolls and how good they looked.

"We should do that," I said. "We gotta get some shirts and start throwing our own parties."

All the girls agreed, but the problem was that only Tee and I had houses with basements and both of our mothers were strict. I couldn't imagine my mother letting me have a party with all of those kids in our basement. And drinking and smoking? That was out of the question. But we'd figure that out later.

"The first thing we have to do is start collecting money so that we can buy shirts," Kris said. "We can get shirts, pops and pluggers."

"Yeah, that will give us time to work up to having our own parties. We don't have to have them right away because we're gonna have to have enough money for a DJ, too," Nessa said.

By the time we made it home, we'd made plans to collect dues and we talked about how we would have to work up to having the parties. We were all going to have to figure it out together, but we had time because we had to save a lot of money to save all the money for what we wanted to do. But we had a plan and I was excited about it.

When I got home, my sister was on the porch. "I see you made it home on time," she said.

"Yeah," I said, glad that the fight made the party end early.

"Good, 'cause you know you got to get up for church in the morning."

My sister didn't have to tell me that. I went inside, and got everything ready for church and in the morning, I was up and ready before my mother. She was so surprised when she came out into the living room and I was already there.

"I'm happy to see you up," she said.

I wanted my mom to be in a good mood. I was going to have to keep her that way if I wanted to ever have a party at our house.

About a half hour later, we were all at church. This was going to be the first time we'd be singing with the new choir director, Danny. He had started working with us a few weeks before and I thought he was cool. He was young, in his thirties, I thought. He was dark-skinned with a Jeri curl. I liked that he made choir practice fun and short. Because I always had to go to a party right afterwards and my girls would have left me if I was late. So I liked that he never kept us in practice too long.

At his first choir practice, he had all of us sing and then he put us into groups. I was an alto, with my kinda low voice and my sister was a soprano.

The whole time he led us singing this morning, he kept staring at me, but I was used to it. He did that at practice and I didn't really think anything of it. I liked that he was the new director.

That Sunday, we returned home and chilled like every other Sunday and then, it was back to school Monday. I was happy to discover that we had a substitute teacher in Ms. Moore's class. I loved it because time went by real quick.

When the bell rang and I was on my way to Mrs. Crowder's class, when I saw Kris and Moore talking in the hallway again. This time, it was Moore who called me over. "Hey Shawnda, I have someone I want you to meet."

"Who?"

"My brother?"

"Your brother? What's his name?"

"Rambo."

I laughed at his name. "Rambo?"

"Yeah, he's on the football team with me. He's one of the star players. You've got to meet him."

Since he kept pressing me, I said, "Okay," and then, he walked away.

When he was far enough so that he wouldn't hear me, I said, "Why did you let him do that?"

"What?"

"You know I don't know how to talk to guys."

"It's not a big deal. Just talk to him."

"Okay, but before Moore introduces us, point him out to me first 'cause I'm scared."

She shook her head. "There's nothing to be scared about, but okay."

Just as she agreed, Selina came rushing past me. "Come on," she said. "We're gonna be late."

We ended up doing our usual run-walk to the other building, up the stairs and then we got to Mrs. Crowder's class just in time. When we walked into the classroom, it seemed a little different. Mrs. Crowder was quiet, sitting there just sipping her coffee as she graded papers. As she graded each one, she passed it to the student. Kids were sitting in the class, talking loud and Mrs. Crowder didn't say a word.

What was going on? Something was wrong, but I couldn't figure it out. So I stayed quiet.

When she called me up for my paper, I was almost scared to look at my grade. But, when I saw the 'D', I was relieved. My mother told me not to bring home another F and so this D was better than that.

After she gave out all the papers, Mrs. Crowder stood up, gave us our homework and then, she dismissed the class.

All of us walked out of there so fast. We had never had a class like that with her. But I was just happy with my D.

For the rest of the day when I went into the hallway to go to the next class, I kept hoping that I wouldn't see Kris or Moore.

I couldn't stop thinking about Rambo and how I was scared to see him.

On the way to study hall, I told Selina about what Moore had told me earlier and how I was afraid to meet Rambo.

"Why are you scared? You might like him, Shawnda."

I didn't know how to get her to understand that I wasn't like her. I was still a virgin and I wasn't into guys the way she was. She was still messing around with Herman, but now, she liked another guy, too—Jujuan, this guy who was in the band.

When we got to study hall, Selina and I were trying to read this book from Mrs. Moore's class because I was sure she would be back in class tomorrow. But the whole time, I kept thinking about this Rambo guy.

I was so glad when we got out of school and I didn't see Moore or his friend. I met up with all my girls and on the way home, they talked about their favorite subject—boys. Today, though, they talked about their dicks. Big dicks, little dicks, good dicks, bad dicks. Like I always did when they talked about these things, I was quiet. I didn't know about no dicks, but what they were saying was kinda funny.

Then Michelle said, "My boyfriend gave me crabs."

While all the rest of them said, "No way," "Are you kidding," "Really?" I wanted to ask what the fuck were crabs.

They went on and on about their stories. Just walking home, I was learning a lot of shit.

Sherice noticed that I was quiet and I guessed she wanted to include me. "You're gonna do it soon, I'm sure," she said. "Just know that when you do it, it's gonna hurt so just be ready."

They kept talking, I kept listening and we all kept laughing. When we got to the block where we all went separate ways, Michelle said, "Everybody do your homework real quick so that we can meet back at Kris's house. 'Cause we have a lot to talk about...homecoming."

"Yeah, homecoming," they all said.

This was just one more thing that they knew about that I didn't know. But if it was anything like the pep rally, I was all in and I couldn't wait.

Just a couple of hours later, we met back at Kris's house and my friends did all the talking again while I just listened since they were talking about homecoming. They talked about the dance and what we all had to wear, and how we had to do our hair. They were talking about all of these girly things and even though I was in high school, I was still a tomboy. I wasn't into all of that kind of stuff—especially not makeup.

Kris said, "You're going to wear makeup for the dance, Shawna."

"Noooooo," I said, shaking my head. "I don't like makeup."

"How do you know if you've never worn it?" Kris asked.

That was a good question, but I just knew.

Kris said, "Just wear lipstick and liner."

"Shit, what else is there?" I asked.

Coco said, "There's foundation and blush and eyeshadow."

Wow! I never paid attention. I didn't know it was all of that.

"I'll think about it," I said because I knew if I didn't agree to it a little bit, they would never leave me alone.

We hung out a little bit more and then, when I left and walked home, all I could think about was homecoming. This sounded like it was really going to be a big deal. When I got home, I went into my mom's room.

"Ma, homecoming is coming up."

She smiled. "That's always fun. That's the kind of things that are fun in high school."

"I need a new outfit for the homecoming dance."

"When is it?"

"This Friday."

"Okay." She nodded. "Come straight home from school tomorrow and we'll go downtown."

"Thanks, Ma."

I was so excited, so you know I was home on time the next day. My mom and I got on the green line bus to head downtown to Carson's. I picked out a pair of black Guess jeans with a yellow and white striped top. I also got a yellow sweater to go over my outfit and then black patent leather shoes.

Back at home, I called Kris, excited to tell her about everything my mom bought for me.

"We did, too," she said. "We went down to 63rd. We called you, but your brother said that you had left already."

"That's cool. That means everybody is set for the dance."

"Yup," she said. "Shawn almost got caught, she was trying to steal too much stuff. You know how I do...I like to get in and get out, but she was taking too long. I was going to leave her." Kris laughed. "She can't come with us next time."

Kris went on and on, and she had me laughing, too.

When we hung up, we both agreed that we couldn't wait for Friday. I had a feeling things were going to be different for me.

Chapter 8

The next day, we all walked to school together, but Nessa was mad at everybody for what happened when they'd gone down to 63rd Street.

"Y'all were going to leave my cousin, Coco out there like that?" she asked.

I stayed out of it because I wasn't there. But Nessa was really mad.

"All of y'all are phony 'cause y'all all talk about each other behind everybody's back."

Wow! I was surprised she said that. That was when I knew she was mad for real.

She said, "Tee talks about everybody and Michelle does, too."

We all looked at each other, wondering who was saying what. This had taken a bad turn and now, I was in it. I said, "Whoever has something to say about me, y'all need to say it right here."

When nobody said anything, Nessa kept talking saying all kinds of things. And then she added, "And Shawnda, they said you're just a dumb virgin."

I glared at Tee and when I asked her if that was true, she started stuttering. "No, it was just a joke."

That was when Michelle's funky-smelling ass spoke up. "I didn't say nothing about nobody. It was Tee, not me. I was just laughing at what she said."

"Well whether you're talking about me or laughing at me, it's all the same thing," Sherice said jumping in everybody's faces. "I'll beat your little ass 'cause I don't like you no way. Can't nobody talk about nobody 'cause nobody is better than any of us. So let this shit come up again and I'm beating your ass."

I was right with Sherice. I couldn't stand anyone who was a back stabber.

So everybody was mad at each other all because of the one I called, Stutter-Box. As far as I was concerned Kris, Sherice, Nessa and I were still cool. But when we got to school, Tee and I just walked past each other like strangers.

When I saw Selina in Mrs. Moore's class, I told here what went down and she couldn't believe it. "I don't like none of them anyway," she said. "Except for Kris. All the rest of them are shitty acting."

Once we settled down in class, Mrs. Moore handed out our exams and once again, I'd gotten a D. I was happy; this had to mean that I was catching up, even just a little.

At the end of Mrs. Moore's class, Selina and I decided that we weren't feeling Mrs. Crowder today, but on our way to study hall, we saw Kris near the locker room and she was waving like she wanted us to come over to her. Selina and I ran over to her and when we got there, she said, "Look to your right. The guy talking to Moore is Rambo!"

When I glanced at them, all I could do was smile. Rambo was fine. He looked like an athlete with his muscular arms and thick thighs. But it was his smile that I noticed the most. It lit up his whole face. He really was handsome.

"Girl, you better jump on that," Selina said. "He's cute."

"Yeah," I said. "But let's go before Moore sees us."

"What? You don't want to meet him?" Kris asked as if she couldn't believe me.

"Not now. Another time." I grabbed Selina's hand and we scooted off to study hall.

For the rest of the day, I couldn't even focus. I was already behind in all my classes and trying to catch up. But it was hard to pay attention because all I could think about was Rambo. all I did was think about Rambo. On our walk home, Selina wanted to talk about him, too.

"So what do you think?" she asked. "Do you think you and Rambo will get together?"

"I haven't even met him yet." Then, I added, "But I'm interested. He is cute."

While Selina kept talking about how I needed to get with him, I kept thinking about how I was interested, but I couldn't imagine that he'd be interested in me. There were lots of cute girls in school and I didn't look like any of them. I was so skinny, even though I did have big titties. My breasts were the biggest things on me. But besides that, I wasn't very curvy, I didn't have a big butt. I was nothing like the things guys seemed to like. And then, I still had lots of acne. That hadn't gotten any better at all.

So while I wanted to meet Rambo, but I was really worried, that he wouldn't be interested in me.

At our splitting off point, I told Selina that I would see her tomorrow and then continued my walk home alone, still thinking about Rambo. When I got closer to my house, though, I slowed down a bit. I saw my sister, Mia outside, talking to this guy who was sitting in a brand new Cadillac. Even from far away, I could tell that he had money because of the way he was dressed and all of the diamond rings and gold chains that he wore.

They were talking and laughing and I didn't think I'd ever seen my sister carrying on like that. Slowly, I walked past her and when she finally noticed me, Mia said, "Oh, hey, Shawnda. I'll be up there in a little while."

"Okay," I said with a grin. I went inside, but waited right in the hallway, peeking through the door, watching them.

Finally, she stepped away from the car and waited for him to drive away before she came into the house. When she saw me standing there, she cracked up and I laughed, too.

"Girl, who is that?" I said.

"That's Red."

"He sure is sharp." Then, I asked her, "Is he your boyfriend?"

She nodded. "Yeah, but don't say nothing to nobody," she warned me. I knew what that was about. Ma was strict with all of us, even Mia, even though she already had a baby. Maybe that was why our mother was so strict. So I knew Mia didn't want any drama with Red—at least not yet.

We all hung out for the rest of that night at home, eating dinner, doing our chores and then playing with the Atari my mom had bought us. With only two remotes, we had to take turns, but we made it work.

It was pretty late when Selina called me and told me she wasn't going to be in school the next day because she had to do something with her mother. So I called Kris and told her not to leave me in the morning.

But when Kris and I met up the next day, I was shocked to see Michelle. I couldn't believe they were meeting up at Kris's house as if nothing had happened.

When I walked up, I didn't say anything to either of them. But Michelle spoke to me.

"Hey, I like your skirt," she said.

"Thanks."

That was it. For the rest of the walk to school, I was quiet. Kris did all the talking and it was so awkward between us. I was glad to get to school, just to get away from them. But then, in my classes, I really missed Selina. The day felt like a blur without my friend, until I came out of one of my classes and there was Kris and Moore in the hall waiting for me.

Kris said, "Walk with us."

"Okay," I said, not anxious to get to my next class anyway.

But we'd only taken a few steps before Moore yelled out, "Yo, Rambo."

The guy I saw yesterday was standing just a little bit in front of us. He turned around and smiled, making me feel better than I'd felt all day. But I was nervous when he walked to us and I was really nervous when Moore introduced us.

But then, Rambo smiled at me and all I could do was grin right back at him. We talked for a little while...or really, it was Kris, Moore and Rambo talking. I was too shy to say anything. Rambo did try to pull me into the conversation. He was soft spoken and very playful and he did make me feel at ease. He talked to me as if he liked me already.

Then, Moore said to me, "We're going over to Kris's house later so meet us over there."

"Okay, I'll be there."

Rambo nodded and stared at me. Then, his smile got even wider. "I'll see you there."

I turned and rushed away, but I was blushing hard because of the way he looked at me. It was like he saw *me.* Like he was looking past my acne and my skinny ass. So, I felt a little bit better. Wait, that's a lie—I felt a whole lot better and I couldn't wait to see him.

I rushed straight home from school so that I could get ready for getting together with Rambo at Kris's house. At home, I changed my clothes, brushed my teeth, did what I could with my hair and then hurried over to Kris's house.

When I got there, she grabbed my arm and pulled me inside. "Girl, you need to put on some lipstick and eye liner."

"How am I supposed to do that?" I asked. "I don't know how."

"Don't worry, I'll help you."

She took me into the bathroom and then hooked me up. Once she finished, I looked in the mirror and I have to say, I did look cute. I was still nervous though, and when the doorbell rang, it got even worse.

Kris let them in as if she'd done this a thousand times before and right away, I started smiling. He was dressed in jeans and his football jacket with the #64 on the back, looking even better than when I saw him at school. By the time we sat down in the living room and talked, I finally relaxed. It was easy to be comfortable with Rambo because he was so soft spoken and gentle. We talked and laughed (although it was mostly Kris and Moore talking) as if the four of us had been friends forever and it didn't take me long to feel like I really liked Rambo. There was so much to like about him: his smile was the first thing I noticed and I could also tell that he was a kind guy. What I liked best was that he was so funny. Besides all of that, he was really cute...and every time he smiled, I felt better.

In the middle of our conversation, Moore asked, "Shawnda, you got a boyfriend?"

I shook my head. "No."

Moore said, "Rambo don't have a girlfriend."

I wondered if Rambo was as shy as I was because it seemed like Moore was doing all the talking for him, just like Kris often did for me. That by itself would make us a good match—two shy people together.

"Give her your phone number," Moore told Rambo. After he did, Moore asked me and Kris, "Are y'all going to game?"

"Yeah, we are," Kris said for the both of us.

I smiled and nodded because I couldn't wait. I couldn't wait to go to wear my new outfit and I couldn't wait to go to be there with Rambo.

After a couple of hours, Moore and Rambo got up to go and I was so sorry. But when Rambo said, "I'll see you tomorrow," I felt better.

"Okay."

When Kris and Moore hugged and kissed, Rambo and I just stood there. But when they left, I was so happy. It was time for me to go home because I didn't want to be late. I didn't want to take the chance of messing up and missing out on homecoming.

But before I could go home, I told Kris that she had to help me get rid of this makeup. There was no way for me to go home with it because if my mom saw me wearing lipstick and eyeliner, I would be on punishment for sure.

As Kris helped me, she asked, "Do you like Rambo?"

"Yeah, he seems cool." For some reason, that made her laugh and when she did, I did, too. But then, I added, "I have to be more talkative," I said. "I don't want him to think that I don't like him."

"You will be. Don't worry about it. As you get to know him better, you'll be more comfortable."

When I left Kris's house, I knew she was right and I couldn't wait to see what the future would be like for me and Rambo.

Chapter 9

When I got home, Mia was getting dressed to go out with Red and she looked so pretty. Before she left, Mia asked me, "Can you watch Iris while I'm out?"

I nodded. Of course I would watch my niece. She was only two years old and I loved taking care of her. She wasn't a cry baby, and it was always fun to be around her. So for the rest of the evening, I sat with Iris while I was watching TV. Then, I went into my mother's room and gave her the baby because I had to go to bed.

I'd only been asleep for a little while when I heard a knock on the door. Mia came in and I wondered why she knocked since we shared the same room. She asked, "Is Iris asleep?"

"Yeah, but she's with Ma."

"Can you go get her for me, please?" Mia asked.

I knew why she didn't want to go in there. She didn't want to answer a whole bunch of questions. So I went and got my niece. Iris was asleep, so when I came back into the room, Mia and I could talk.

She said, "I really like Red. And it's not just because he has a lot of money." She went on to describe his big house and all the jewelry he had. "Look what he gave me," she said.

I hadn't even noticed the chain she had on. It was a gold rope necklace with a charm that hung down with her name on it.

"He gave you that?" I asked. It looked really expensive.

She nodded. "Yeah, and he gave me some money, too. Shawnda, he has a whole lot of money."

As she got undressed, we kept talking about how much she really liked Red and how they wanted to be together. We talked until we both fell asleep.

We had talked for too long and too late because when it was time for me to get up, I was too tired. Right away I rolled over. I was going to miss first period; I would just get to school in time for second period. I slept a little more, and then got dressed and hopped on the bus since I didn't have anyone to walk with. The moment I walked through the school doors, I saw Rambo. He was always smiling, but his smile seemed to get brighter when he turned to me.

"What's up?" he said. "You're just getting here?"

I nodded. "I overslept," I told him.

"Okay, I'll walk you to class."

"All right." It was interesting because I always said I didn't know how to talk to boys, but Rambo was so easy to talk to. He was excited about the homecoming game coming up and he told me how much he liked playing football. I told him that I couldn't wait to see him play.

When we got to my classroom, Rambo took of his football jacket. "Here," he said. "Wear this for the rest of the day."

"Okay." I put on his jacket like it was no big deal, but I was frantic. I was wearing the star football player's jacket!

"I'll catch up with you later," he said.

I said, "Okay," again and went into Mrs. Crowder's class.

When I walked in, Selina took one look at me and started laughing. "I guess y'all finally met, huh?" she said.

"Yeah, yesterday."

"Ah shit, y'all fucked?"

"Hell nah," I said. "I told you, I just met him yesterday. Like, really, Selina?"

"I'm just asking 'cause me and Jujuan be getting it in."

"Where?" I said.

"At his house. Sometimes we do it before school and sometimes we do it after."

"Oh," I said. "Well, I am no where near ready for that. I can wait; I'm really not in a rush to have sex.

"You don't even know what you're missing."

I shrugged and sat down in class. I didn't know why all of my friends were in a rush for themselves, but I definitely didn't understand why they were in a rush for me.

I tried to focus in class, but of course, my mind was on Rambo. After class, I ran into Kris and when she saw me in Rambo's jacket, she started smiling so hard.

"How you get his jacket?" she asked, sounding like she was surprised.

"He saw me coming into school and gave it to me. I'm gonna give it back to him after last period."

"If you wear it all day, everybody's gonna be looking at you," Kris said. "Because he's a star player."

I just shrugged as Kris and Selina walked off to their next class and I went to study hall. But Kris was right. Everybody stared at me, but no one said anything, though I was waiting for somebody to say something. For the rest of the day, I just kinda wandered through my classes, not really pay attention. I was so bored, I decided to just leave early. I wanted to get ready for the Homecoming dance anyway.

I was half way home before I remembered that I had on his jacket. Well, I wasn't going all the way back to school; I'd just catch up with him later. But he caught up with me first because Kris called me and told me that Rambo was looking for me.

"Give him my address," I told her.

I was excited about seeing him again, but when he knocked on the door, I didn't know why I felt shy again. I had Mia pass him his jacket through the door so I didn't have to talk to him.

"Who was that?" my sister asked.

"Just a guy from school." I didn't want to tell anyone that he was the first guy I had ever liked.

For the next few hours, I got ready. My outfit was all ready and then, I curled my hair because for the first time, I wasn't thinking about being a tomboy; I wanted to look extra pretty. So that meant that I wanted to put on a little makeup, too—just lipstick and eyeliner like Kris had put on me the other day.

Then like we always did, we all met up at Kris's house to walk to the dance together. I still wasn't speaking all that much to the other girls, but things had gotten a little bit better. Especially once they took one look at me.

"Are you wearing makeup?" Michelle said.

"Yup." I grinned.

"I can't believe it," Sherice said. "But you really look pretty."

"Thanks," I said.

"Yeah," Michelle added. "It looks so good on you. You should wear it more often."

They made me feel good and that kinda broke the ice between us, so we talked all the way to the dance. Before we even stepped inside the gym, we could hear the music. It was bumping so loud. We walked inside and like the pep rally, it was packed, although no one was really dancing. Everybody was just standing around talking and laughing.

There were so many people there, but most of them were people I'd never seen in my life. But as we walked around, there was only one person that I was looking for and I didn't see him or Moore. I wondered what happened to them? That was a little disappointing because the whole time I was getting ready for the dance, I was thinking about Rambo. I wanted to look cute for him.

But I wasn't going to let not seeing him stop me. I was with my girls and I was going to have a good time. There weren't very many people on the dance floor, but that didn't stop Michelle. She was always dancing and she was jamming now. We hung out talking to the people we didn't know and my girls introduced me to a lot of people they knew but I didn't.

When the lights flashed a few hours later, I couldn't believe the time had passed so fast. We piled out of the building, but then there were so many kids outside. There had to be hundreds. I was surprised to see the police there, trying to direct the crowd.

"Go home," they kept saying. "No hanging out, no standing around. Just go straight home."

I guess they didn't want any fights to break out. We walked back together, talking about the dance and how much fun we had. We all stopped at Kris's house and one of her mother's friends was sitting on the porch, smoking weed. We walked up the steps and sat down with her.

"Y'all want some?" she said as she offered the joint to us.

"Yeah," we all said.

I didn't smoke, but all my friends did. But tonight, I decided to try it. I took a pull and had to cough a bit, but then, I got used to it. After a little while, we started laughing and talking loud.

"Be quiet!" Kris's mother's friend told us. "Y'all better quiet it down. I don't want anyone else to come out here."

We worked hard to keep our giggles inside because we didn't want Kris's mom coming out to the porch. I was sure she wouldn't be happy at all about what we were doing. She didn't want all of us teenagers smoking weed on her porch.

We stayed for a little while longer before Tee and I walked home together. But it was hard for us because with just those few pulls, we were both so high. When we got to my house, Mia and Red were outside. I stumbled up the porch steps and then laughed. The two of them looked at me.

"You're high," Red said.

"Nah!" I giggled.

"Yes, you are," Mia said. "Your eyes are half closed and I can smell the weed. You better change your clothes as soon as you get upstairs."

"You can smell it?" I asked, so surprised.

"Yeah!"

"Okay," I said. That straightened me up a little. I rushed into the house and went straight to my room. Thank God my mother was in her bedroom, with her TV blasting so loud. I changed my clothes so fast, putting on a pair of shorts and a T-shirt. Then, I hid what I'd worn to the dance under the mattress. I'd keep it there until the morning when I could wash my clothes myself.

I plopped down on my bed. Wow, that was close. I didn't know that you could smell weed and I didn't know that weed made your eyes kinda closed. Thank God only Mia saw me. I was so tired, but I was really hungry. I went into the kitchen and found a cold ass piece of chicken in the fridge. But I was so hungry, I didn't care. I really didn't like the way this weed was making me feel and so after I ate, I drank a lot of water. But that didn't help. I guessed the only thing was for me to go to bed.

All I knew before I closed my eyes was that I didn't want anymore of that shit. That was enough weed for me.

Chapter 10

The next morning, I tried to beat everybody up so that I could wash first, but Mia was already up washing.

"What are you doing up so early?" I asked her.

"I had to take care of this 'cause me and Iris are going over to Red's for the weekend."

"Oh, wow. You told Mama about him?"

She nodded. "Yeah. I was glad to get that over with." Then, she turned the conversation to me. "What made you smoke last night?" She sounded surprised and I understood why. I didn't normally do things like that.

"I don't know. I guess since everyone else was trying it, I didn't want to be left out. But I didn't like it."

Mia nodded like she understood, but then, she shook her head. "I didn't like it either. I tried it once and it made me feel paranoid."

"Well, I won't do it again," I lied.

"Good. Don't."

Once Mia was finished washing, I was next. For the next couple of hours, I did all of my chores and got my clothes ready for the week. By the time my mother came in from the store, I had done everything I was supposed to do.

When my mother saw me, she said, "Hey, how was the homecoming dance?"

"It was really fun, Ma. I really enjoyed myself."

"That's good, baby."

For the rest of the day, I chilled out. I don't know why I was being so laid back. Maybe it was because of the weed last night. But I didn't do anything for the whole day and even the next day, I was up and ready for church even before my mother.

When we all got the church and stepped inside, the first person I saw was Danny, the choir director. When we walked into the vestibule, there he was staring right in my face. He looked at me for a moment and then, he turned away.

"He's a creep," I whispered to my sister.

"Who?"

"Danny. He keeps staring at me."

"I thought you liked him."

"I did when he first got here. But in the last few weeks, he's been creepy."

She looked over at him. "I think he's all right. He may just be a little weird."

She was right about that. when he first came, I liked him because he was fun. But then over the last couple of weeks, he changed. He started just staring a lot. Even when I caught him looking at me, he wouldn't turn away. He didn't care that I caught him looking at me that way. I just wanted to get away from him.

I couldn't get away right now, though. We had to sing for church. I followed my sister into the choir stand and when the service began, we sang our songs. Well, I didn't really sing. I didn't like being in the choir, so I just moved my lips. Even though I was only pretending to be singing, I still had to watch Danny since he was the one leading us, but as soon as we stopped singing, I turned away from him. But every couple of minutes when I peeked at him, he was looking at me.

He just kept staring at me through the entire service while the preacher preached and while they passed around the offering plate. I kept turning away but every time I turned back, his eyes were on me.

I was glad when the service was finally over and just as I was heading toward the door with my mother and sister and brother, I heard someone calling out to me.

"Shawnda, wait."

I turned around and there was Danny. When he caught up to me, he asked, "How is everything going?"

"Pretty good." I was trying to be polite because we were in church and that's how my mother wanted me to be. But I really didn't like talking to him. Not even when there were a lot of people around.

"You look nice today."

"Thank you." I really didn't want to talk to him, so I was just trying to give him the shortest answers that I could.

"So, you're in high school, right?"

"Yes."

"What year?"

"Freshman."

"How old are you?"

"Fifteen." I kept answering him, but damn, he asked too many questions.

Then, he turned to my sister, I guess because he didn't want it to be obvious that he was just talking to me. He asked her the same questions, but then, my mom cut in.

"Let's go girls," she said and I hurried out the door.

As we walked back to our house, my mother said, "Y'all sang really good today."

I looked at my sister and we cracked up because she knew that I only moved my lips. At home, it was a pretty normal day. Just eating and chilling. A couple of hours after we got home, we heard music blasting from the street. We rushed to the window and saw Red pull up in his Cadillac. He was bringing Mia home.

My sister and I rushed downstairs to talk to them. I really liked Red. He was always so cool and this day wasn't any different. He and Mia got out of the car, came up to the porch and he just hung out with us for a while. Then he asked me to go to the store for him.

"Get me some orange juice and chocolate chip cookies," he said as he pulled a whole bunch of money out of his pocket.

We went to the store and when we came back, he told us to keep the change. After a while, Red said he had to leave, but he told Mia, "I'll be back for you and Iris in a couple of hours."

"Okay," she said before they kissed.

It seemed like we were going to be seeing less and less of Mia since she really was now with Red. When we got upstairs and Mia unpacked, I saw all of these new clothes and shoes and she had tons of jewelry.

Wow! I was happy for my sister. She had a cool boyfriend who had a cool car. As she unpacked so that she could pack again, we sat on our beds and talked.

"He has a lot of money, doesn't he?" I said, even though she'd told me this before.

"Yeah, I think he's doing something illegal."

"Really?"

"Yeah, but don't say anything."

I promised her that I wouldn't because if Mama found out, she wouldn't like it at all. Especially not with Iris being around all of that. So I kept my sister's secret.

Chapter 11

I woke up that Monday for school with a feeling that I hadn't had before. I was excited about seeing Rambo. I don't know how, but we had somehow missed him and Moore at the homecoming.

Today, I wanted to take the bus, so once I hooked up with Kris and Selina and I paid their fare. When we got to the school, we ran into Pam and Novella, two girls that I'd met in my classes. My social circle had been growing since I'd been at Robeson for the last several months. It was good to have friends outside of the Q Girls.

Pam and Novella were really cool, though Pam was a little stuck up. But not Novella. She was straight gangsta and loved to fight. She would argue with every damn body and she'd fight over any damn thing. Watching her made me understand how my mother felt when I was in elementary school and would fight all the time.

When we walked up to the school, the first thing Novella said to me was, "You go with Rambo?"

"Yeah, I do. Why? What you hear about him?"

"Nothing." She shook her head. "He's really quiet, and I didn't know. I just saw you with his jacket on one day."

"Well yeah, I really like him."

"He's a star football player so I say go for it."

"Yeah, but all of that doesn't matter to me. I just like him 'cause he's cool." I didn't add that every time I saw Rambo, his face would light up when he saw me. That would make me blush so hard and make me feel so good.

And he was easy to talk to because he was shyer than me sometimes. But he was funny and smart and thoughtful and so respectful. We didn't get to do a lot of different things together, but we would hang out. Besides being at school, Rambo would come over to my house and we would sit on the porch and talk for hours. When we weren't together, we'd talk on the phone. No matter where we were, though, he was always the perfect gentleman.

I didn't know a lot about boys and I had never had a boyfriend before, but it felt like I was in love with Rambo already. I always thought about him. It didn't matter if I was in school or at home, he was always on my mind. He was the only reason why I loved going to school now, and I knew that was a damn shame. But he got me to school, and would carry my books and walk me from class to class.

That's why when after a few weeks of us going together when I got to school and didn't see him, I was confused. We always met up. I waited all day and didn't see him and that was the longest school day I'd had in a long time. When I got out, I tried to call him, but whoever answered his house phone said Rambo couldn't receive any phone calls.

So, I couldn't wait to get to school the next day, but the same thing happened—Rambo was a no show and I didn't know what to do. When I asked Kris if she'd seen Rambo, she told me what happened.

"No, he's been suspended and he's on punishment."

"Suspended? Why?"

She shrugged. "I don't know. Something happened."

"So how long?" I asked, not knowing what I would do if I couldn't see him.

"I don't know, but I'll ask Moore if he knows."

"Okay. Thank you."

She looked at me. "Damn, girl. You really miss him, huh?" she teased.

We laughed and then went to class, but I had to push myself through the whole day again. When I got home, I did my chores and didn't even ask my mom if I could go outside. Even though I talked and joked with my sister, I was feeling really sad. I didn't know why. I guessed I really missed Rambo a lot.

The next day in school, Rambo was still missing, but when I saw Kris in the hall, she said, "Girl, there's this guy that I want you to see. He's so fine."

"Who?"

"His name is Chevy. You gotta see him. Meet me here right after lunch," she said.

"Okay," I said.

When we hooked up after lunch, Kris pointed out this little light-skinned boy who had finger waves in his long hair. He was walking around carrying a pair of drumsticks and that made me crack up. Kris laughed with me and we laughed for so long, that it wasn't about Chevy anymore. That's just how it was with us. We laughed so much together, sometimes, we didn't even know what we were laughing at.

But when we finally stopped laughing, Kris said, "Ain't he fine?"

I shook my head. "No Kris. Not to me."

"Shit, you're crazy."

"Have you even talked to him yet?"

"Not yet. But I will."

"Well what about Moore?"

"We're still cool."

When she didn't add anything else, I left it at that with Moore. I told her to just let me know when she talked to Chevy.

"Okay," she said. And then, my friend walked off with the biggest smile that I'd ever seen.

❧

I met up with Selina and Renee, but the day dragged on. I guessed it was that I was still thinking about Rambo. I wondered when he'd be back in school.

Before the day ended, Kris found my ass again in the hall between classes. She said, "Girl, I met him and he got a friend."

I raised my eyebrows. "A friend for who? Selina?"

"Nah, you!"

Like earlier, I started cracking up and Kris laughed with me. I said, "You already know who my baby is."

"I know, but I just don't want to be by myself when he comes by my house."

I was thinking here we go again. She did this to me with Anthony. I told her, "I have to get to class. I'll see you later."

But the next day, Kris wanted me to meet her by the lunchroom at lunch time. I didn't know why I agreed. Even though I was seeing Rambo, I was still shy. But like the last time, I was going just to help my girl out.

When that time came around, I walked up to the cafeteria and Kris and Chevy were there. She introduced me to Chevy and then, Chevy introduced me to his friend. I stood there and the four of us talked, though I wasn't really interested.

But then, out of the blue, I saw Rambo. He was standing across the hall staring at me. At first, I smiled. I was so happy to see him, but the smile that he always had on his face when he saw me wasn't there. He didn't smile at all. He had a look of disgust on his face.

Oh my God. What did he think was going on? When he turned around and walked away, I wanted to go after him, but I felt like I was frozen. I didn't know what to do, but I was dying inside. I was so glad when the bell rang and we all walked off.

I was so nervous and sad. I kept trying to think of what to do. When I got to the class, I talked to Selina and told her what happened. "He saw me with Chevy and his friend and what if he thinks that something's going on?"

"Just talk to him," she told me. "Just tell him what happened."

I took a deep breath. "Okay," I said.

I looked for him during our next break and when I saw him, once again, the smile was missing from his face. That made me so nervous because I was so used to his smile. That was what I liked best about him.

But at least his eyes stayed on me and I tried to gather up the courage to speak to him. When I stopped in front of him, before I could say anything, he lifted me up, turned around and dumped me into the garbage can. I couldn't believe he'd done that to me.

Kids who were in the hallway were cracking up. I was so embarrassed, but more than that, I was mad and I was sad. Why would he do that to me?

I couldn't even get out of the garbage can by myself. People passing by had to help me out. There was no way I could stay in school after that.

All the way home, I was thinking about what he'd done to me. I kept going back and forth between mad and sad. When I got into the house, the first thing I did was call him. I kept calling, but he was in class and then, he had practice afterwards.

I called and called and called and Rambo never called me back. I couldn't believe it. He wasn't even giving me a chance to explain.

I called Kris, wanting to talk to her about Rambo, but she was excited. "Listen, Chevy and his friend are coming over...."

I was already saying no in my head.

She continued, "Friday after school and I don't want to be here...."

I knew what she was going to say. She didn't want to be there by herself. So I told her cool, I'd be there. It was going to be fine anyway. I was sure that I'd speak to Rambo and I'd be able to fix it with him. I would just talk to Chevy's friend because I could tell that Kris really liked Chevy and she was my girl. We did whatever we could for each other. She always had my back and I wanted to make sure that I had hers, too.

It was going to be fine because by Friday, I would be back with my baby.

Chapter 12

No matter what I did, I couldn't get Rambo to talk to me. He wouldn't return my calls, and then, when I saw him in school, he wouldn't even look at me. I would try to make eye contact, but he wouldn't. And if he looked at me by mistake, he definitely wouldn't smile. After a couple of days, I stopped even seeing him in the hall; he was completely avoiding me.

I didn't know what to do. How could I make him talk to me? It seemed impossible since I could tell that he was so disgusted with me, maybe he even hated me. So after a few days, I just gave up and left Rambo alone.

By Friday, I was just going through the day. I didn't like school at all without Rambo, but it seemed that was how it was going to be from now on. That Friday evening, like I promised Kris, I got to her house around five and she was so excited. "Girl, you have to put on some makeup," she said. "Just lipstick and eyeliner."

Even when I was feeling good, I didn't like wearing makeup. But I put on a little make-up so that Kris would be happy.

When Chevy and his friend arrived, we all sat down and talked. Chevy's friend introduced himself as Dee and then asked me, "You stay here?"

"No, I live over on Halsted."

"Oh, across from the car shop?"

"Yeah."

And that was it. All the rest of the talking was between Kris and Chevy. I guessed Dee was here for the same reason that I was here—he was only doing a favor for his friend. That weekend, we all hung out at a party at the Courtyard. It was my first time being there and when we walked up to the place, I knew there was going to be a lot of people inside. There were so many cars, more cars in one place than I'd ever seen. Then, when we walked in, it felt like the whole damn school was there. It was massive with young people and older people. The music was blasting and with the loud music and all of that noise as people talked and laughed, we could hardly hear each other. There were too many people there for me.

And when you had that many people, of course, fights broke out. There were rival gangs and girl fights. They were fighting all at once and I was like, what the hell is going on? But with the GDs and the BDs in one place, I knew something was bound to jump off.

It was a hot mess and if my mom had found out that I was up there in that craziness, she would have killed me, brought me back to life, then killed me again. It was fun to hang out with everyone, but it was too dangerous.

After a couple of hours, Kris and I hopped in the car with Chevy and Dee and they wanted to go to Dee's house. Going to his house was cool with me, I still had a little more time before my curfew and it was better than being at the Courtyard.

When we got there, we went into Dee's bedroom and he and I sat on one bed and Chevy and Kris got on the other bed. While Chevy and Kris started kissing, I wasn't sure what I was supposed to do. Dee and I tried to talk a little, but then, we started kissing.

I think the only reason we kissed was because we were there and just needed something to do. I didn't really know what I was doing and Dee guided me. When he started unzipping my pants, I whispered, "I'm a virgin."

"That's cool," he said, as he undressed.

I was so nervous, but really, Dee just did it all. There was nothing good about having sex with him. It hurt so much and I was sweating so badly. I was glad when it was over.

When we finished, I couldn't believe it. I couldn't believe what had just happened. When I put my clothes back on, I told Kris we had to go. She said, "That's fine," and she asked Chevy to drive us home.

I couldn't wait to get in the car. I was so mad and hurt at what I'd done. I kept asking myself why had I done that? I didn't even like this guy. We didn't have anything in common, we didn't know each other since we didn't even talk.

Kris and I got in the back seat as Dee and Chevy sat in the front. When he started the air, I whispered to Kris, "Can you tell that I had sex?"

She stared at me for a moment and then started laughing. "Are you for real?" she asked.

"Yes," I said. I was for real. I remembered how Mia could tell that I'd smoked weed and I didn't want that to happen to me now. "I'm scared to go home. My mom's gonna kill me." That's how naïve I was.

"Just act normal," she said. "No one will be able to tell. I wouldn't have known if you hadn't told me."

I did what Kris told me. When I got to my house, I just went to my room, took a shower, and then got in my bed. The only person, besides me and Dee, who would ever know what happened was Kris. I wasn't going to tell anyone at all!

Except at school on Monday, I told Selina. Why did I do that? With her loud ass, she laughed so hard. "I can't believe you did that?"

Shit, I couldn't believe it either. But it was done and that was that. That was what I kept telling myself, but I really did feel so ashamed.

That afternoon, Moore met up with me in the hall. "Hey Shawna," he called out to me. "Are you talking to Dee?"

My heart started beating fast, but I said, "No, why would you say that?"

"Rambo told me. He said he was at the Courtyard and he saw y'all together and then he saw y'all leave together."

Oh my God! Rambo was there? I didn't see him with all of those people around me. "No! I'm not talking to him," I said. "We just needed a ride home." But even though that's what I said, I knew that I had fucked up with the boy that I was in love with.

This was a mess because I didn't have that much time left with Rambo. He was graduating in June and he would be off to college in Alabama to play football. But it didn't seem like I was going to need time because from that day on, Rambo didn't speak to me. When I figured out that he was avoiding me, I started avoiding him, even though that really hurt me. I avoided Dee, too. I didn't want to have anything to do with him.

That worked for a few weeks, but then, one day, Kris convinced me to go to band. "You've been cutting it all year, just come to class."

"No. I'm going to fail anyway."

She kept pushing me and then, I did what I always did—I gave in. But when we got to class, I couldn't believe it. I looked up and there was Chevy...and Dee. I had done everything I could to avoid him and now, here he was sitting in my class. I didn't want to see him.

The kids in class were doing some line dance, so I went and sat in the back. I didn't know why I was mad at Dee. I was mad at myself for being stupid. I fucked up with the love of my life. As soon as the bell rang, I was out of there. Kris wanted me to wait for her, but I knew if I did, I would end up talking to Chevy and Dee. So I got out of there.

I had planned to walk home by myself, but I caught up with Nessa. As we walked, she said, "Shawnda, I got something to tell you."

"What?"

"I'm pregnant."

"Really?"

"Yeah." She told me that her mom knew already and she'd told her boyfriend and everyone else.

I didn't know what to say. I asked, "When are you due?"

"I have to go to the doctor next week. Then, I'll find out."

"Well, the good thing is that school will be out in a couple of weeks, so you'll have no worries."

"I'm not worried," she said, surprising me a little 'cause I would've definitely been worried. "I'm just nervous," she added.

I understood that, this was a big deal. When we got to our splitting up point, I told her to take care and then, I walked the rest of the way by myself. I didn't know why, but talking to Nessa made me think about Rambo. I was so mad at him, even though what happened was my fault. But I kept thinking about him, even when I got home. I just sat around, thinking about how much I really loved Rambo.

Kris called later that afternoon and said, "Guess what?"

"What?"

"Rambo is dating someone else."

"What? For real?"

"Yeah, Moore told me."

I was so hurt by that. When I hung up, I went into the bathroom and just cried my eyes out. I couldn't believe how much

I had messed up big time. Now, I knew it was completely over because I was so dumb and stupid.

Rambo was a good guy, even my mom loved him because she said he was so nice and respectful. But finally, I got over my tears. I was still heartbroken because I had fucked it all up. But I knew that we paid for our mistakes. All I wanted to do was to learn from them, too. One thing I knew for sure I would never let anyone know how much I was hurt. I was going to play it strong and pretend that I was okay. I was going to have to find a way to block out the good times Rambo and I had spent together and for the next couple of weeks, that's what I did.

But it wasn't as easy at night. That pain would sneak up on me and my ass would tear up so fast. It was easier during the day because I could stay busy enough to block thoughts of Rambo out of my head.

The weeks began to pass and I couldn't wait for summer. I was hoping that we'd have so much fun that I'd forget about Rambo all together. That was my plan.

Chapter 13

Summer was here, school was out and I was so happy. Not just because I wouldn't have to go to class, but because I thought it would be easier to put Rambo behind me. He'd gone to his prom, graduated and now, he was off to college. That was the good thing, I guessed. The bad thing...I got all Fs.

I was going to be in trouble with my mom again, but worse than that, I was going to be a demo. I remembered my friends telling me after my first set of grades to make sure that I didn't do that—I didn't want to be a sophomore with freshmen classes. Well, I was going to be a sophomore with freshmen classes. Of course, I was the only one. Everyone else passed.

That was a sad day for me. Not only because I was being left back again, but because my bad grades reminded me of Rambo.

"You need to go to class, Shawnda."

In my head, I could almost hear Rambo's voice telling me to do what I should have done. I didn't know what I was thinking. All I had to do was go to class, do the work and pass a simple test. It wasn't that hard; it was just that I didn't like it.

I promised myself that next year, I was definitely going to do better. I had to. The big problem I had now was that I had to tell my mom about my grades. Shit! That wasn't going to be easy. But I didn't want to spend a lot of time worrying about it. So I just went into her bedroom and did it.

She looked so sad, so disappointed in me, and I felt so bad. But I was going to feel worse because then she started lecturing me about how I should want more out of life and how I needed to listen. She went on and on, it was a hard speech and it really hurt like hell to hear. Everything she said, though, was right. I knew that. I did have to learn and I was going to try my hardest to make a change in my life and it was going to start with this summer.

I was able to get a summer job working at one of the grammar schools tutoring kids and just overall helping them with their schoolwork. I was happy; at least I wouldn't be broke because my mother wasn't giving me any money. Not after all of those failing grades.

Summer really wasn't that different than being in school. During the week, we'd hang out at Kris's house to chill and then on the weekends, we partied. Our friendship dynamics were changing. I guess when you got older, you just naturally drifted apart. So while Kris and I were still best friends, and Michelle had other friends. Nessa and Sherice were pretty much loners anyway. But when we all got together, it was cool.

My mom didn't let me go to all the parties, but that was fine with me. I didn't care as much. I was going to work every day, meeting different people, and trying to do right.

One of the right things that I was trying to do came from my mother. "Make sure you save money out of every check. Put it away for a rainy day."

My mother had some sayings, but as I got older, I understood and saw that she was right.

But still, I liked the nights when I partied with my friends. On this particular Friday, we all decided to go down to 63rd Street to get outfits to wear. When we got down there, we stole our jeans, but bought our shirts. What was crazy about that is we all had money; this was something that we just wanted to do.

That night, we got to the party, all of us looking good, smelling good, feeling good. The house was packed, as usual. It seemed as if everyone from the school was there. Like always, the music was loud and poppin' and we had so much fun. When we walked out, there were a lot of police around. That had started happening at the big parties, which I guess was good so that fights wouldn't break out.

Kris and Chevy were still talking, but the rest of us were ready to go. As we were standing there waiting for Kris, Dee came over to me.

"I haven't seen you in a while."

"Yeah," I said.

"You wanna come over to my house?"

"No."

It wasn't that I just didn't want to be around him, I was supposed to be home by ten and it was already after ten. He just shrugged and I began to walk with my friends. As we were walking, one of the other kids yelled out, "There's a party over on Lowe."

"Oh, let's go over there," Kris said.

Everyone was for it, but not me. I was already late, so they all walked me to my street and then they went on to the other party. I was glad when I got home and my brother, Dell was there to let me in the house. I was glad because if I had to wake my mother to let me in, there would've been a whole lot of trouble.

My mother proved that to me the next day when she asked me what time I'd come home.

"About ten-fifteen, ten-thirty. The buses were running slow."

That wasn't a good enough excuse for my mother. "When I say ten, I mean ten. If the buses are running slow, then leave earlier so that you'll get home on time."

"Okay, Ma," I said, knowing that she meant every word.

But that didn't make me change my behavior. A few weeks later, when Kris told me there was another party on Lowe, at first,

I didn't want to go because like I told Kris, most of those parties had too many guys. I liked parties that had a better mix.

We went to the party anyway, and had a good time. When my friends started smoking, I took a couple of pulls on a joint, too. I still didn't like the way weed made me feel, but since my friends were doing it, I did it. I didn't think about what smoking would mean until I was almost home, and then I remembered what happened last time.

This time, when I got to the porch, it wasn't Mia who was there. This time, it was Dell and as soon as I walked up to the porch, my brother said, "You been smoking?"

Damn! Weed really was bad, it told on you all the time. I told my brother, "No. We were at a party and there were a lot of people there who was smoking so I think the smell got in my clothes."

I didn't think he believed me, but he said, "You better not be smoking," he said. "Put your clothes on the back porch to get the smell out."

"Okay," I said, then rushed upstairs. I changed clothes, did what my brother said, then got my clothes ready for church in the morning.

One thing was for sure—no matter what was going on in my life, I always had church. It was my mother's rule, so we always had church in us. But it wasn't just the teachings of my mother or the church that guided me. My grandmother, Madea was also a person who instilled a lot into me. She preached to us about everything in life. She taught us about Jesus, told us to listen to our mama, talked to us about always having the right attitude and about being kind whenever we could. Every time my grandmother spoke to us, I knew where my mother got her long lectures from—her mother. We were getting double doses of everything between the two of them.

Of course, I always listened politely, even when I didn't want to hear what she said or when I didn't want to answer the questions she asked.

"What are you going to be when you grow up?"

My dumb ass always answered, "I'm going to be a doctor or a lawyer."

My grandmother always gave me the same look—like, girl get the hell out of here. Then, she would laugh so hard, but in the end she'd tell me to just do the best that I could.

It was a blessing that my other grandmother, my father's mother, was in our lives as well. Big Mama always put in time with us, and especially during the holidays, she made sure that she bought us plenty of birthday and Christmas presents.

Although there were men in my family, my brothers and one uncle, I was mostly surrounded by strong women. Even though I didn't always act like it, I really had learned a lot from all of them. And I was going to need every single lesson that I learned.

Chapter 14

I couldn't believe that it was time for school again. That was a quick summer and now, I as a seventeen year old sophomore. Before our classes started, Kris and I headed down to 63rd to "shop" for school clothes. Of course we stole some, and paid for some. That's just what we always did.

Kris and Chevy were still going strong and at the end of the summer, I started hanging out with them and Dee. I wasn't into him; he and I never even had a real conversation. We didn't have anything in common. But we got together and had sex. For me, it was whatever.

There was proof of that when one night, Kris and Chevy and Dee and I had sex in the same room. Our nasty asses didn't even care. It was dark and afterwards, we just all got dressed and they took us back to Kris's house and I walked home from there. Kris was into Chevy, but I was never into Dee and he wasn't into me. We just did whatever.

Before school started, there was a going-back to school party at the Courtyard, so we all decided to go, even though we weren't as close as we used to be. It was going to be good to see everybody I hadn't seen over the summer.

Like every other party, especially the ones at the Courtyard, everybody was there, the music was fire, people were drinking and smoking...and there were fights. There was one literally in front of us and the police had to break it up. It was the last big celebration before school on Monday.

I promised myself that this year, I was going to do better. I felt like I was as old as fuck, yet I was a sophomore demo. I had to focus and get it together. My plan was to always go to school, no cutting classes, always do my homework. I really did want to make my mama proud and I was going to do it right this time.

There was one thing that made me sad about going to school—it was Rambo. I still didn't really understand how I'd messed up like that with him. It was so stupid and even though I tried, I still thought about him, and it still hurt a lot. I was just flat out dumb, but I had to find a way to get over this, too.

That first day at school was really different than first day last year. I wasn't lost like I'd been back then and with my new plan I went to every class, took notes and then went home. I was proud of what I'd done my first day, but when I got home, I wasn't feeling well. I figured it was all the effort I'd put in during that day. So, I just got into bed. I was just going to sleep for a few hours, but I ended up sleeping the whole fucking day. When I woke up, I was pissed. Now, I was going to be up all night.

I got up and ate, but then, I was shocked when I went back to bed and I actually slept. The next morning, I felt a little better. But after I got up, took a shower, and brushed my teeth, I threw up. I guessed I still wasn't feeling well. I grabbed a piece of bread, and some orange juice and rushed out to go to school. It wasn't until I was halfway there that I realized I hadn't done my homework. Damn. I was trying to do the right thing, trying to get on the right track, but I'd slept the day away. I was mad at myself, but I wasn't going to give up.

At school, I talked to all of my teachers and asked if I could bring my homework in the next day. Again, I went to every class, took notes and paid attention. Two days in a row, except for homework, I was off to a good start.

I was happy about that.

❧

When I got home from school, my sister and her boyfriend were sitting on the porch. Mia had pretty much moved in with Red, so we didn't see her all that much. Things were going really well with the two of them. Red was always sharp and what I liked was that he kept Mia and Iris that way, too. He was giving them the finer things in life and I really liked him for doing that.

"Hey," I said to them as I walked up the porch steps.

After we talked for a little while, Red held up his car keys. "Here, you can drive for an hour and bring the car right back."

"Really?" I grinned. I had just learned how to drive.

"Yeah," Red said. "Just bring the car bring it back in an hour.

"Okay," I said, so excited. I hopped in that car and drove to Kris's house. When I honked the horn, she came running out.

"Oh my God," she said.

"Get in," I told her. "Red said that I can drive for an hour."

She got right into the car and we turned the music up loud, blasting hip hop through the streets. Even though I knew how to drive, I didn't have a license. But if Red didn't care, I didn't care. We drove all through the city, past Hamilton Park where we hung out for a little while, and then, we drove by Robeson. All the kids were gone, though, so there was no one to see us.

When it got close to an hour, I didn't even play around. I wanted to get this car back to Red on time and I was glad I did.

Red nodded when I handed him back the keys. "Okay," he said. "Next time, you can drive it for longer since you came back on time."

It had been an exciting afternoon. Kris headed home and since I had homework, I went inside and sat at the kitchen table.

As I opened up my books, Dell came into the kitchen and stared at me for a moment.

"Shit," he said. "I ain't never seen you do no homework."

We both laughed.

"You hungry?" he asked.

"Yeah."

As I sat there and focused, he fried me a hamburger and poured me a glass of Kool-Aid. It wasn't until I started eating that I realized how hungry I was. I hadn't eaten all day. But after eating, I went back to my homework because I was committed this semester.

The next morning before I left for school, my mom came to my bedroom. "You feel okay?"

"Yeah. I'm fine."

She nodded. "Okay I just want to make sure because you slept all day yesterday."

"I wasn't feeling well." I shrugged. "But I feel better now."

She stared at me for a little longer before she said, "Okay, go on to school."

I didn't tell my mother about my goal to do better this semester. I just wanted to do my work and prove it to her to make her proud. For the next couple of weeks, I kept the same schedule. I went to school, I took notes, paid attention, did the school work and I didn't cut class or play around at home. When I got home, I did my homework, staying focused and determined. There were days, though, when it was hard because I'd been getting sick so much and I wanted to sleep a lot. But even with that, I kept my focus. When grades came out, I was so excited. I was confident that I had done so much better.

But then, I got my grades: I had all Ds, except for an F in math. I was so disappointed. How had that happened? I really thought I'd been doing something.

When I told Kris, she said, "That's okay, you still have time to make it up. Just work harder."

"Yeah, right," I said. I wasn't convinced. What more could I do?

Then, Kris looked at me and busted out laughing. I didn't know what was so funny. Was she laughing at my grades? "What?"

"You're gaining weight."

"No, I'm not," I said. "I never gain weight." That was the truth. I'd been so skinny my whole life. Nothing I did ever helped me to get bigger.

She said, "Yes, you are."

"No, I'm not. I've just been sick. I haven't been feeling all that well."

Kris's eyes got big. "Sick? Girl, you ain't sick. You're pregnant."

"Hell nah!"

She crossed her arms. "Okay. Have you had your period?"

"Nope, not yet."

"Shawnda," she squealed my name. "You're pregnant!"

She said it as if she was so sure and now, she scared me. Could I be pregnant? Was that why I was so sick? "Don't say that," I told her. "You know my mama would kill me for real. I can't be pregnant, Kris. No!" I felt like I couldn't breath and I started having heart palpitations. There was no way this could be happening. But Kris was right. I had been getting bigger.

The next day, I had to drag myself to school. I was upset with my grades and I was scared that I was pregnant. At lunchtime, I was so hungry that I went into the lunchroom for the first time. I was in line when Dee came up to me.

He didn't say a word to me at first, just touched my stomach. "You pregnant?"

I narrowed my eyes as I looked at him. "How did you know?"

"Just looking at you, I can tell. Plus, Kris told me."

If my best friend had been standing there in front of me right now, I would have killed her.

He asked me if I'd told anyone beside Kris and I told him no. "I haven't even told my mama yet."

He frowned as if he thought that was so strange. "Why not?"

I told him, "I don't know," but the truth was, I was too scared. She was going to be so disappointed because one of the talks she had with me and my sisters was about getting birth control so that we wouldn't get pregnant. I knew my mother loved Iris even though Mia had gotten pregnant in high school. But my mom really wanted us to do more than that.

I hadn't planned for this to happen at all; it was just happening so quickly.

Now that Kris knew and I was gaining weight, I knew I had to tell my mom soon. It was just so scary. So when I got home, I told Mia first.

"Wow," she said. "Well, you better tell Mama, 'cause you're gonna have to see a doctor."

"Okay, but I'm scared," I said. "Maybe you can help me. How did you tell her when you were pregnant?"

"It was hard, but you have to tell her," my sister said.

I knew she was right, but I just couldn't do it. I struggled with this for weeks. I stayed sick and hungry and I slept all the time. Mama kept asking me questions about why I was sick or why I was sleeping and I kept making up different lies. I started eating at school or Kris's house. I did anything and everything possible to keep this secret from my mother, even though I was gaining weight.

A few weeks later, Mia came over with Iris and we talked for a while before she said, "Did you tell Mama?"

I shook my head. "Nope. Not yet."

"Shawnda! You have to hurry up and tell her because I can see a difference in your face and you are gaining weight."

"I'm too scared!"

"Just do it while no one else is here." Then, she did something I didn't expect. She called out, "Ma, come here."

My heart jumped out of my chest.

When my mother came into the living room, she looked at Mia. "What?"

Mia said, "Shawnda has something to tell you."

Then, I said the ultimate words: "I'm pregnant."

My mother just stood there, staring at me for what felt like five minutes. It probably wasn't that long, but it felt that way. Finally, she said, "You're jiving me."

"No." I shook my head.

"Well," she said. "I bet Rambo is happy." My mother really liked him.

I lowered my head when I said, "No, Ma, it's not Rambo's."

My mother was shocked and speechless. After another few moments, my mother did something that I'd never seen her do. She cried. She put down the food she was eating and went into her bedroom.

When she walked away from me, I felt two feelings at once—I cried. I was so hurt because I had hurt her. But at the same time, I felt relief. It was like a weight had been lifted from my chest.

At the same time, though, this was a crazy situation. I was pregnant by someone I didn't even know well. He was someone that I didn't even talk to, only occasionally when we wanted to have sex. We were truly nothing more than fuck buddies and now we were going to be parents.

Chapter 15

When my mother finally came out of her room, she sat down and talked to me. "How did this happen, Shawnda?" she asked. "Why did you let this happen?"

I didn't say anything.

She continued, "I told you to let me know when you wanted birth control," she continued her lecture. "We sat and talked about this more than once. I always had the door open."

Finally, I said, "I know, Ma. It all happened so quickly. It really just happened."

She was silent for a moment before she shook her head. "Shawnda, it's hard taking care of a baby. It takes a lot of love and patience and it comes with so much responsibility. It will change your life." She sighed. "But I'm here for you. We'll make a doctor's appointment." Then, she got up and as she walked out of the room, she said, "I can't believe my baby is having a baby."

A few days later, she made an appointment with the University of Chicago Medical Center. It was the first time that I'd been seen by a female doctor.

She was pleasant as she said to me, "Get undressed and then sit on the bed there."

I undressed, put on the paper robe and then when the doctor told me to lay back and put my feet in the stirrups, I was like, "What?"

She repeated what she said and I was so scared. But I did what she told me to do. Then, she said, "I'm going to insert a speculum into your vagina."

I looked at that weird silver metal thing. "You're putting that where?"

Again, she had to repeat what she said. "I'm inserting this into your vagina so that I can take a look inside, and take some tissue samples." I must've looked real scared to her because she added, "Just think of this as a penis."

A penis? Was she kidding me? A penis was soft. This thing was hard and when she put it inside of me, it was cold and very, very uncomfortable. Then, when she took it out, she put her hand inside of me. All I wanted to do was get out of there, but next, she asked me a whole bunch of questions:

"When was your last menstrual cycle?"

"When was the last time you had sex?"

"Did you have unprotected sex?"

The whole time she was questioning me, all I could think was WTF? I was so glad to get out of there.

When we got home, my mother just looked at me and shook her head. "If you think that speculum was uncomfortable, wait until you have a baby. In eight months a whole baby's body will be coming out of you."

The good thing was that the doctor told me I didn't have to go back to see her for another two to three months. I'd be going back for an ultrasound, whatever that was. Then, the visits would be every month until in the final trimester, I'd be seeing her every two weeks. I was so glad my mother had been with me and would be with me throughout all of this because I felt so clueless and helpless.

But my mother started telling me things that I hadn't thought about. First, she told me that I needed to go to Zayers and put baby clothes on layaway. "If you start doing that now, when the baby comes, you'll have everything you need."

Then, she asked me, "Have you told the daddy yet?"

"Yeah," I said.

She didn't ask me who it was. She just said, "Good, because you're going to need him."

When my mother left me alone, I was thinking at least that was done. One down and I ha two more to go—I had to tell both of my grandmothers. Even though I didn't want to disappoint them, I knew talking to them would be easier than talking to my mom. It was so hard with my mother because she'd been the one who'd tried to put me on the right path with all of her speeches and lectures. She had been trying to teach me to do right, but I just hadn't listened and not listening was what got me here—broke and pregnant.

I called Dee and told him to come over so that we could talk. He showed up a few hours later and when he walked into my house, the first thing he asked was, "Did you tell your mother?"

"Yeah."

"So when is the baby coming?"

"September fifteenth," I told him.

And that was it. We didn't talk about anything else. He left; I didn't even bother to introduce him to my mother. I barely knew him myself.

After all of that, what I needed was a friendly voice, so I called Kris and told her what happened with the doctor.

She said, "You'll be all right," as if she understood everything that I was going through.

"I know, but I'm still scared." Then, I asked her, "Have you seen or talked to Moore?" What I really wanted to know was if he'd said anything about Rambo.

She told me that she had spoken to Moore and that Rambo lived in California now and was going to be a daddy himself.

"What? Really?"

"Yeah," she said. And then, she turned the subject to, "Are you going back to school?"

Even though I was on the phone, I shook my head. "Nah," and then I told her goodbye. I knew she probably thought that I would come down to her house, but I was too embarrassed to go outside now. I was getting bigger and bigger and soon everyone would know that I was a pregnant teen.

Before the news hit the streets, I wanted to make sure my siblings knew. I told my big brother, Dell first and at first, he was shocked. Then, I could tell that he was hurt, but I knew he would stand by me. I told all of my other siblings too. Just like Dell, they were all really surprised and they were hurt; but just like my mother and grandmothers, I knew everyone would be in my corner. I was their sister and they would help in any way they could.

That night when I went to sleep, my mind was filled with all the things that had happened that day. It finally hit me that my life was about to totally change. The worst change was that there would be no chance for me and Rambo now. I'd lost my high school sweetheart. The first boy I'd ever loved and probably the only one I ever would was gone forever.

When I closed my eyes, I could still see Rambo's smile and the look in his eyes whenever he saw me. No one lit up like that and I missed him in my life so much. But there was no need for me to keep thinking about him. He was gone and with what was going to happen in my life, I needed to get over it and just move on.

Now that I wasn't going to school, my days consisted of sleeping, eating, shopping for my baby and then sitting on the front porch with Mia. My sister always made sure that I sat on a pillow.

"You have to do that so you won't get hemorrhoids," she told me.

I didn't know what that was, but it sounded bad enough, so I always sat on a pillow like she told me to do.

A few days later when I was sitting in the living room just watching TV, I heard a car door in front of our house slam. At first, I wasn't even going to get up since I was sure it was my sister and Red. But I decided to get up and peek through the window.

"Oh shit," I whispered to myself. It was my grandmother. I needed to hide. That was a crazy thought, but I meant it. Like I said, telling my grandmother would be easier than telling my mom, but it still wasn't going to be easy. My grandmother was going to be so disappointed. Right now, I really didn't want to see the hurt in her face that I saw in everyone else's.

I rushed into my bedroom, laid down on the bed and closed my eyes. It took my grandmother a few minutes to work her way through the house. She came into the bedroom, stood over me, and even pinched me. But I didn't move at all. Finally, she went back out to the front of the house and sat with my mother.

I could hear my mom, my grandmother and Dell laughing, and finally I got up. I couldn't stay in my room for the rest of my life; I was going to have to face her at some time. I just needed to get this over with. They were all still talking and laughing when I got to the front room and I just stood there until they noticed me.

My grandmother glanced up, and as she was chewing her gum, she looked me up and down. Everyone was silent until she finally said, "You pregnant?"

"Yeah," I said.

Then, she went right back to talking to my mother and brother. She didn't give me a long speech or nothing. I just went into the living room with them and we all talked and laughed. Boy, I had worked myself up and telling my grandmother was easier than telling anyone else in my family and I was glad about that.

After that, the days just seemed to be the same—eating, sleeping, shopping. The weeks turned into months and finally, one day I returned to the hospital. The sonogram showed that my baby was fine and I was doing well, too. Every month, I visited the doctor so that she could check me out and make sure my pregnancy was progressing normally. One of the things I didn't like was that each time, she weighed me. At one of the doctor visits when I found out I was a whopping two hundred pounds, I was shocked. I had always been the skinny kid, but I guessed that's what eating Kentucky Fried Chicken every single day for lunch and dinner would do.

My mother kept trying to tell me that I needed to eat healthier and I didn't need to each so much. "I cook every day. You better stop eating all that fast food."

She tried to warn me, but I didn't care. All I saw when I looked in the mirror was a fat, greedy, ugly pregnant girl.

As I went through my pregnancy, I separated myself from everyone. I never wanted to go outside and since I wasn't in school anymore, I was pretty isolated. I even pushed away from Kris. Of course, she was still my friend; she always called to check on me and I was glad about that. And then, one day, she came by to visit me.

We sat on the porch and talked and laughed like we'd always done. I hadn't been that happy in a long time. Oh, my God, I really missed her. She always knew what to say to make me feel good. And she always knew how to fill me in on the drama. All

I could do was shake my head when she told me that everybody was talking about everybody behind their backs.

"I'm not surprised. That's what a bunch of bitches do. All they do is talk because none of them can fight except for Sherice."

"Yeah, you're right."

I said, "Just let me know if my name comes up. I'll beat all their asses, even if I am pregnant."

We cracked up. In the middle of all of our laughter, Kris stopped and asked, "Can I feel your stomach?"

"Yeah."

She stood from her chair and carefully pressed her hand on my belly. "Wow, it's so hard."

"I know, right? It's a really different and amazing feeling, especially when the baby kicks."

She sat back down and asked me if I was scared and I told her that I was. But she told me that I didn't have anything to worry about and that she would be there if I needed anything.

I really appreciated that and I really appreciated her. Even though I was pregnant, she still had my back.

But Kris was the only one that I stayed in touch with. I didn't go out at all. All I did was stay inside the house, eat and wait for the baby to come.

I did a lot of thinking, too. I thought and wondered how in the world was I going to take care of my baby? I didn't have any money, I didn't have a job, and now, I only had an eighth grade education. I didn't really know anything about life, even though my mother had tried to be strict and guide me so that I would have a better life. Now, I thought about all of her long speeches and lectures and I wanted to kick myself in the ass for not listening.

I wished that I could do it all over, but I had made my bed and now, this was my life.

Chapter 16

One morning I woke up a little earlier than normal. I had to go to the bathroom and when I did, I noticed that my urine was pink. I didn't think anything about it, though. I wasn't in any kind of pain, so I thought this was normal. Going back to bed, I planned to sleep, but I kept having the urge to pee. The only thing—every time I went to the bathroom, nothing would come out.

After I'd been to the bathroom a couple of times, I met my mother in the hallway.

"You okay?" she asked me. "I heard you getting up a couple of times."

"I'm okay," I said. "When I peed, it was pink."

She frowned a little. "How are you feeling? Does your stomach hurt?"

I shook my head. "No."

But my mother was still concerned. "Maybe you should go to the hospital anyway."

"Okay," I said, since I didn't know anything about having a baby. I had to find Dee's beeper number, but after looking everywhere for the paper where I'd written it down, I couldn't find it. So my mother told my sister to take me to the hospital, but while she was getting dressed, I found his number in my old pack back.

I beeped Dee 9-1-1 and he called me right back. He agreed to take me to the hospital, but by the time he got there and my sister helped me down the stairs, I was buckled over with a pain I had never felt. I didn't think I would be able to handle this, but I had no other choice.

Dee helped me get into the car and when we got to the hospital, the nurses didn't wait—they took me right to a room to see a doctor. The nurse had me undress, put on a hospital gown and then she checked me.

"You're eight centimeters," she said. "You're almost ready, but we'll just keep you in here."

The nurse left, but Dee and my sister stayed with me. I was so thirsty and they only gave me ice chips and the pain was becoming unbearable. Every few minutes, the doctor who I'd been seeing came in to check on me and after about an hour, she said, "Okay, you're ready."

My sister and Dee stood up as the doctor sat at the edge of the bottom of the bed. "I want you to push as hard as you can until I say stop."

I did what the doctor told me to do, but I thought that I was going to split open with pain. I pushed, but I hollered at the same time.

The doctor said, "Okay, can you do more pushing and less hollering?"

As much as I was hurting, I couldn't believe she said that to me.

She said, "So, let's try again. Push!"

All I could think about was that this shit was hard. I cried, I wanted my mama for real.

"You've got to push," my sister said. "Push, Shawnda and just get it over with. "

I tried to do what my sister said and then, she shouted, "Oh my God, I can see the baby's head." My sister came back up and held my hand. "You just have to push."

With my sister holding my hand, I pushed, and I pushed. I pushed at least ten more times and finally, there he was. My baby boy. As they cleaned him up, I saw blood everywhere, all over the floor, all over the sheets, blood even covered my sister's white gym shoes.

I felt a big relief and I had one thought—I would never do that again.

When they finally brought him to me, the nurse told me he was nine pounds, fifteen ounces and twenty inches long. And right there, I felt better. I was so happy to meet my baby and hold him.

After a while, Dee left, saying that he wanted to buy some things for the baby. I had plenty of stuff: pampers, clothes. But what I didn't have was formula, or even the clothes and blanket that my baby would need to go home. So, Dee went to buy that stuff and he said he would drop it all off at my mother's house.

I rocked my baby in my arms and though I was happy to see him, I knew I wasn't going to have any more kids. When my sister left the room, the nurse showed me how to take care of my baby: she showed me how to feed him and then, burp him and even the best way to hold him. The nurse laid him in a baby cart next to me, and then, she left me alone.

I was glad to be by myself; I was so exhausted and I just wanted to go to sleep. But right before I closed my eyes, the baby started crying. So I took him from the baby cart and laid him next to me. Then, together, we slept.

A few minutes later, the nurse came in and when she raised her voice, I woke up.

"You can't do that," she said, taking the baby away from me. "He can't sleep with you; he could be suffocated."

She seemed annoyed, but I didn't know any of this. Of course, it was all new to me. One thing I noticed the first day was that I cried. I couldn't stop crying, and I didn't know why I was crying. I was glad that everyone kept calling. My mother, my sister and Kris called. My best friend was so excited.

"I'm coming up there to see you," Kris said.

"No, meet me at the house. I'm going home tomorrow."

"Okay, cool. I'll see you then."

I held my baby a lot. He was so handsome to me and I loved staring at him and talking to him. A few hours after he was born, the nurse came in with the social worker.

"So, I want to take care of his birth certificate," the social worker told me. "Do you have a name for him yet?"

I nodded. "He's going to have his father's name." And then, I don't know why, but I busted out crying again.

The social worker said, "Are you okay?"

I nodded, even though I still kept crying.

"Okay, I'm going to give you a few moments, but we're going to need his dad to sign the papers. So have him come up here and sign."

When she left me alone, I paged him again and when he called I told him about the birth certificates and the paper.

"Okay," he said. "When are you going home?"

"Tomorrow."

He told me that he would pick me up and first thing the next morning, he was there. I was so happy because I wanted to go home and see my mama. After Dee signed the papers, he carried my bag while the nurse rolled me downstairs to the entrance. I couldn't wait to get home.

When I got there, my mom and sisters met me at the door and then, my mom helped me to my room.

"Oh, I love it," I said. My mother had decorated my room and it was so cute with baby stuff—clothes, blankets, toys, pampers—

everywhere. My mom had picked up everything I had on layaway and it was all on display.

One thing, I didn't have to worry about what my baby would need. So, I was home, I had my baby, and everyone around me was so happy. So why did I feel so sad?

❧

My first day home, all I did was cry. But I was able to hide my crying from everyone. Whenever anyone came around me, I would just wipe my face and pretend that everything was okay.

I had to do that a lot. All day long, people kept visiting and there were so many who came by. From Kris to my relatives and neighbors, everyone wanted to see me and the baby. They were all so happy to see me and my baby. They talked and laughed and when I was by myself, I cried.

But in front of everyone, I pretended that I was happy. So many people came by our house that my mother finally thought it was too much.

"Okay, no more visitors," she said. "People can come and see you tomorrow."

She cleared out the house and all of a sudden, it was quiet. And that quiet felt so good.

Inside my bedroom, my mother came and sat with me. She held the baby so that I could relax a bit. That's how it was for the next few days. My mother and sisters were there to help me and boy, did I need it.

My baby would stay up all night and cry for hours. My mother, sisters and I took shifts and I am so grateful or else I wouldn't have gotten any sleep. He was a hand-full already, too much for me alone, especially since I didn't know anything.

My mother kept telling me not to worry about what I knew—most of it would come naturally. And in those first weeks, she was right. I learned how to bathe him and prepare his bottle so that it wasn't too hot for him. I learned how to hold him, change his diaper and calm him when he was crying. I settled into motherhood and learned how to relax a little. But it was still tough for me. I still cried a lot.

Everyone said that I was spoiling my baby because I carried him everywhere. After I showered and dressed every day, I held him as much as I could. But I had to because every time I laid him down, he cried.

"You are really going to spoil him and make it hard for your babysitter when you go back to school."

School? I had a baby, how could I go back to school with a baby? I said to my mother, "Can't I just find a job?"

"Yeah," she said. "But for how long?" Before I could answer, she said, "That little job won't get you far. You have a child now; you have to think long-term. It would be easier to finish school now, find a career and then work at that."

"So you're saying that I should get my GED, then go to college or trade school for another couple of years?"

"Yeah, Shawnda, I know that sounds like a lot, but it's better to do this now instead of later. Time flies by fast, trust me. Think about what you want to do, what you like doing. Make some goals and follow through on them."

I said, "Okay, Ma," but that conversation was too much for me to deal with right now. But if there was one thing that I did know, my mama had been lecturing me for a long time and she was always right. I would think about it, but right now, all I could think about was taking care of my baby.

Chapter 17

I felt as if I had no life; I stayed in the house for two months straight, not leaving except for my doctor's appointments for me and Booney. At my six week doctor's checkup, my doctor gave me birth control pills.

"These pills will make sure that you won't get pregnant again."

Oh, I thought. This must've been the medicine that my mother had been talking about.

The doctor continued, "Start taking it the first Sunday after your period."

"Okay, cool," I said. But when I went home, I didn't start taking the pills right away. I wasn't thinking about sex; it was the furthest thing from my mind.

All of my attention was on Booney. Week by week, he was getting so big, but the biggest thing that had changed with him was that he wasn't crying as much. I loved watching him; he played with his little toys and he loved to laugh, but he was still staying up all night long.

I was always so tired and I tried everything to get him to sleep. While the house was quiet with everyone else asleep, I would walk around with him in my arms. That was always a good time for me to think about all that was ahead of me. Whether I was going back to school or going to get a job. I'd told my mother that I wanted to work, but if I did that, who would watch my baby? So much was going through what felt like my unstable mind.

Whatever, I wasn't going to make any decisions right now. My baby was still too young for me to do anything since I had help.

My mother was helping to support me and the baby, so I didn't have to worry about money.

Although Dee and I weren't together, he did come by to visit. One day while he was there, he told me he wanted the baby to meet his family. So I got Booney up and dressed and he took me over to his mama's house. That place was packed. There were so many people there, Dee had so many brothers and sisters. There were a lot of them and I didn't have a clue.

It was something; I had a baby with Dee but we didn't even know that much about each other. Besides all of his siblings, I met his mother, too.

We stayed for a couple of hours and his whole family really loved on our baby. When it was time for us to go, Dee took us home and I can really say that I enjoyed that fresh air and getting out of the house.

But once I was back home, I was back to my old schedule. I relaxed for a little while, then I got Booney bathed and dressed for bed. When he went to sleep, I took my own shower. I hoped to go to my room and just go to sleep, but when I got to my bedroom, his eyes were wide open!

It was like that night after night and that left me exhausted. I still cried, mostly at night. And I was sure that there was something wrong with me. At times, my heart would beat fast and there were times when I couldn't even breathe. When this happened, I learned how to just sit still, close my eyes and calm myself down. It worked most of the time. But it left me feeling crazy.

Because I never left the house, sometimes it felt like time was moving so slow. But I could tell time was passing because my baby was getting so big. He began to sit up by himself, then, he was eating more solid foods.

One night, when Booney was almost a year old, Kris called me one night.

"Girl, can you get a babysitter for tonight?"

This was the first time Kris had called me to ask me this. "Why?"

"Well, there's this party tonight..."

"Hold on," I said. "Let me ask my mom."

As I put the phone down, I was excited. I hadn't done anything since my baby was born. It would be good for me to do something except be around my baby.

When I found my mom in the kitchen, I told her, "Kris is on the phone. Can you babysit Booney? There's a party tonight."

"No," my mom said.

I couldn't believe she said that. "Mama, please," I begged. "I haven't been out of this house. I haven't done anything since I had Booney."

"No," she said again and that was it.

"Why? I just want to go out for a few hours."

"No, Shawnda. I'm not going to be to be babysitting for you unless you're going to school or to a job."

I stood there for at least ten minutes and just begged and begged and my mother told me no over and over again. Finally, I went back to the phone, but I'd taken so long, Kris had hung up. I was so sad. My life had changed completely—this was a big lesson learned.

So all I could do was grab my baby and take Booney into the living room with me. This night was going to be like all the other nights—I was just going to play with him and watch TV. A couple of hours later when I heard a knock on the door, I was so glad to see Mia and Iris. At least while they were there, I was able to get a break. Mia held him and Iris played with him for hours. Even though I was still sitting right there in the house, I needed that break.

I sat and talked to my sister for a long time. We didn't get to see each other that much anymore since she and Iris moved out, so I really enjoyed her that day.

Finally, she put Booney on the floor and while Iris played with him, Mia sat next to me. She asked, "So what are you going to do?" she asked me. "Go to school or go to work."

"I'm going to get a job."

She shook her head. "Well, if you get a job, you should go to school, too."

Wow, that was what my mama said, too. Everybody wanted me to go to school. I guessed that maybe I should listen.

❧

The day had come. My baby was one year old. I couldn't believe it. He was really growing up. I wanted this to be a party that everyone would remember, so we had balloons made and bought a cake with his name on it. I invited everyone to come to the party and people showed up from both sides of his family. All of my friends were there: Kris and Chevy who were still together, Nessa, my cousins, some neighbors. I was overwhelmed by the turnout.

Between all of the people and the food and the talking and laughing, the party was really nice. I hadn't had such a good time in a long time. But that good time came with a price because when everyone left and it was time to clean up, there was a lot of work to do. There was popcorn and chips everywhere, all over the floor. I wiped down and cleaned up everything, even taking out the garbage that was filled with boxes and boxes from all the gifts Booney had received. He had so many gifts, I didn't know what I was going to do with everything.

The great thing about the party was that it had worn Booney out. He'd had a good time playing with his toys and the balloons and all of those people. After I bathed him, he was knocked out and I was glad. Right when I got him down, Kris came back over to my house, so I asked my brother Dell to watch Booney while I sat outside on the porch with Kris.

My best friend and I sat on the porch and talked like it was old times. We caught up and as I sat there, I couldn't believe how much my life had changed.

She asked me, "So are you having sex?"

"Hell naw," I said. "I don't want no sex."

We cracked up. Then, I asked, "Have you heard from Moore?"

"No."

"Well, if you do, don't forget to ask him about Rambo."

"I won't. But what about Dee. I thought y'all were together."

I shook my head. "We're not. We just had a kid together. But nooooo! We're not together."

"You better be taking your birth control pills."

That's exactly what my mother had told me. She'd said even if I wasn't having sex, I needed to have those pills in my system so that I wouldn't get pregnant. "I take the pills," I told Kris, "but sometimes, they make me feel really sick."

She didn't ask me any more questions about that and then, just as she was getting ready to leave, Mia drove up in Red's Cadillac. "What's up, Kris?" she asked my friend. Then Mia asked me, "Where's Booney?"

"He's in there asleep. Dell's watching him."

"Okay, you wanna go out?" She held up the keys to the car. "You can go out and drive around for a little while, but come back in an hour."

Hell, yeah, I wanted to go out. I grabbed the keys from her and Kris and I jumped in the car. I was just going to drive around, but it felt so good to get out. The first thing I did was drive over to Rambo's house. I didn't expect him to be there, but I was kinda hoping. But no one was outside, so we just rode around until it was time to take the car back. I wanted to be on time so that Mia would let me drive the car again.

When we got back to my house, Kris hugged me goodbye. And then, I stepped inside and reality hit me. I was a mother and my life was really different.

Chapter 18

Booney was older and I still wasn't doing shit with my life. I felt like a bum since I wasn't working, wasn't going to school. I just stayed in the house and watched my baby and television all day. Every day my life was the same thing: I got up, got dressed, got Booney dressed, we ate, then I laid around. In between, I would cry because there were times when I was just so sad.

It got to the point where I had to do something and I began thinking about school. What did I have to do to get my GED? I looked into taking classes at KKC which wasn't far from my house. The class would be four hours a day, so I began to think, maybe this was something I should do.

Once I had all the information, I talked to my mom. "I'm thinking about taking classes so I can get my GED," I told her.

That's all I had to say. She was so happy. "Sign up for the classes," she said. "Get started."

So, I took my placement test which helped to determine what level I was at and what classes I would need. Then, I got my class schedule and started the following Monday. I was so excited that first day. My mom had agreed to watch Booney like she always promised she would do if I would go to school.

"Just come straight home afterwards," she told me.

I told her I would, but every day after school, I never came straight home. I would hang out with the other students for a little while, just talking to people who were my age instead of to a baby. Every day when I came home, Booney was already fed and dressed. From there, I would take him outside to give my mom a break.

We got into a great routine and it wasn't just my mom by herself. Dell helped, too and so it was easier on all of us with the three of us helping. Every morning, I would get up and eat, then get Booney's clothes out for the day before I left for school.

For the first time, I was kinda enjoying school. I went every day, not like when I was in high school. I didn't miss my classes. I was learning and doing well, but I wasn't ready to take the test. It was because of math—that subject was a bitch. I couldn't get that shit for nothing.

But after a year, I took the test. I failed the math and science part, but the good news was that I only had to retake those two classes. I was determined to put in the time and study a little longer. I was going to do everything to pass.

One day, though, when I got up and got into my routine, I ate, got out Booney's clothes, but right before I got to the front door, I felt the nausea rising up inside of me. I turned around and ran to the bathroom, lifted the toilet lid and threw up.

Right away, I started crying. This couldn't be happening to me again. I wasn't even seeing or going out with Dee. We'd only had sex a couple of times when he came by to see Booney.

There was no way I could go to school that day. I went over to Kris's house. She let me in right away. When I told her what was going on, she stayed home from school, too, just to be with me. I stayed at her house for the rest of the day and just slept until it was time for me to go home. The first thing I did was check out my birth control. I had three missed pills. I took one of the pills I missed and just kept thinking, "I can't be pregnant."

But deep down, I knew. My period hadn't been regular and I just thought it was because the birth control pills had messed with my cycle. I was pregnant...what was I going to do?

This time, it didn't take me long to go in and tell my mother. I didn't stress over it at all. A couple of days later, I just went into her room and said, "Mama, I'm pregnant."

She just shook her head a little. "I knew it," she said and I could tell by her tone that she was so mad at me. "I heard you throwing up two days in a row." She didn't say much else—I guess there was nothing to say.

The next day, my sister came by to tell me that she was pregnant. "Me, too," I told her, thinking that I was a little excited now. My sister and I would give birth close in time.

"Did you tell Mama?" she asked me.

"Yeah, I didn't wait this time."

"Well, I'm going to wait a couple of days." My sister looked at me and shook her head. "Wow, Shawnda. You're gonna have two kids."

Yeah, the thought of that was tough. Two kids. Mia picked up Booney because I needed a break. There was so much on my mind. It was amazing to me how much I'd messed up my life. It started by not listening to my mother and then, not doing what I was supposed to do in school. Even after I had Booney, I hadn't really done anything since I was always putting things off, always thinking that I had plenty of time since I was so young.

But like my mother always said, time really did go by fast and it was moving by me. And this wasn't just about me anymore; I wasn't doing right by Booney because I wasn't building any kind of future for me, so that meant that I wasn't building any kind of future for him.

I had a headache since I'd found out that I was pregnant and I was just miserable. But I had no one to blame but myself for my downhill spiral. No one to blame for me having another baby with a man I'd barely had a conversation with.

I was depressed and the depression stayed with me. Even though Booney was up and walking, I could have gotten a babysitter and found a job, but I was just laying around getting lazier and lazier. I didn't even bother to take the last two parts of the test for my GED. Maybe that was my way of punishing myself because I was so disgusted with what I'd done.

The good thing was that I did have a little more help with Booney now on both sides of his family. But even though there were times when I didn't have my son with me, I didn't use that time wisely. I was about to have a second baby, so my mind was only focused on having all the fun I could before my baby was born.

So whenever Booney wasn't with me, I hung out, driving my sister's car around, and going to parties. The only responsible thing I did was put clothes on lay-away for my baby so that when she or he was born, at least they'd have that.

But even though I was smiling and trying to have fun, in the back of my mind, I felt useless and worthless. I truly thought of myself as a bum-ass bitch, since I was acting like one. I was stuck in a box. Or like I was in a game of Monopoly where no matter what I did, I couldn't pass go. It was hard for me to put one foot in front of the other as I was going down this path of nowhere.

Why didn't I listen to the lectures my mother gave me? Yeah, I was tired of listening to her, but what she told me was true: "Shawnda, if you will just finish school and find a career, you will be set for yourself and your baby. I know you feel like you're at square one, but that's okay. You can start over, it's never too late."

I kept telling her, "Okay, Ma. I'll look into some options."

After I talked to her, I did do what I said I was going to do—I looked into options. But then, I did something else that I always did—I put everything to the side and didn't follow through. I was going to have to stop that if I wanted to do something with my life. But now, I was going to have to wait until after my second baby was born.

Chapter 19

On February 13, 1990, my baby girl, Toota (that was her nickname) came into the world. She was the prettiest little thing with big beautiful eyes and a head full of black hair. I couldn't wait to get her home. But when I got home, boy were things different. It was a struggle juggling two kids: feeding one, bathing the other. My mind was a wreak.

My mother told me, "You might have to get on welfare until you can get yourself together and do better for yourself. Once you go for your six-week checkup, you can go and apply with Social Services and apply for welfare and WIC."

I told her okay, even though I didn't know what WIC was, but I knew that I had to do what my mother suggested, now that I had two babies.

While it was hard on me, it was hard on my children, too. I felt sorry for Booney, feeling like he didn't have much of a chance to be a baby. He didn't seem to take too well to having a little sister at first and not only that, he wasn't developing the way he should.

"He should be talking better for his age," the pediatrician said during one of our doctor visits for Booney. "I want you to talk to him and not using baby talk."

I told the doctor that I would do better, but it wasn't just me. Mia and Iris babied him a lot. So it was an uphill battle for me. But I made it, I did it, and finally by the time Toota was one, Booney was speaking better and she and Booney were getting along fine.

Not only that, my life was changing, too.

"I heard of a school over in Oaklawn that might be good for you," she said.

"What's the school for?"

"A medical assistant. It's only a year's program, but I think this could be good for you."

My sister was right; this did sound good. A medical assistant was the kind of career my mother was always talking about. So once I decided that I wanted to look into this, my family all jumped in to help me. My mom and Dell babysat for me, while I went to class every single day. It was a struggle for them, but they wanted me to finish this class really badly...and I did!

A year later, I was so proud of myself, and everyone in my family was proud of me, too. Finally, I was going to have a career as my mother hoped and what was most important, I would be off of welfare.

Before I could begin working full time as a medical assistant, I had to do something called an externship, where I'd be working at a clinic to get practical experience for a month. I was excited; I wanted to get hands-on experience, but when I got to the clinic, I got a big surprise.

The instructor said to me, "You'll be working here for a month, but you won't get paid."

My face dropped. I wouldn't get paid? I didn't know that. I was so ready to get a paycheck so that I could begin to take care of myself. That was a bummer, but when I told my mother that I wouldn't be paid for thirty days, she understood.

"That's what an externship is all about. It's just about you getting the experience and when you're done, you'll be able to start working in your career."

I was so happy to have my mother's support and for the next thirty days, I worked as hard as I ever had, learning everything I could. I learned about EKGs, how to give injections to patients, how to take a patient's vitals. It was the longest month ever, but it was very interesting work and I did it. I really wanted to do a good job, and it seemed as if I did because after one month when the externship was over, the clinic hired me permanently. I was so happy. This was an accomplishment for me and for everything that my mother had been trying to tell me.

While I went to work, my mother and Dell watched Booney and Toota. For the first time, I felt like I was doing something with my life. I got up every morning with a purpose and then every two weeks, I got a paycheck. That alone made me feel grown up. I guessed I had been grown for a while since I was a mother of two kids, but now, I felt like I was grown mentally, too.

With my first paycheck, I offered my mom and Dell money for taking care of Booney and Toota, but neither one of them would take the money. My mother said, "I want you to save your money so that you can get yourself together."

And Dell told me that all he wanted were a couple of records. So, since they didn't want to take money, I bought my mom things that I knew she'd like such as Harold's Chicken or honeybuns. I bought her lots of Snicker bars and she loved her RC Cola. I got my brother his records. I also got my kid's clothes out of layaway (I was the Queen of Layaways) and I bought them a couple of pairs shoes. I didn't have to buy them too much. Between the money my mother gave me and the things that their dad bought them, I didn't have to spend all of my money taking care of them, which was good.

I was keeping a hectic schedule. Working all day, then coming home to the kids was a lot for me to handle. But now, I was going to have someone else in my corner.

Kris called me, "Guess what?" Before I could answer, Kris said, "I'm pregnant." She was so excited. I was so happy that my kids would have someone to play with besides each other.

"You know what we should do?" Kris said. "After my baby is born, we should get an apartment together."

I was excited about that idea. Kris and I had always talked about getting a place when we turned eighteen and now we could do it. When we'd come up with this idea when we were in school, I didn't think either one of us thought that we'd have babies, but at least, we'd be able to help each other out that way. I couldn't wait for us to do this.

Chapter 20

Kris and I were so excited. We'd found a two bedroom apartment right around the corner from my mom's. So I was still close, but I was on my own—a mom with two kid and Kris had her daughter.

Neither of us were working, we were both on assistance, so that helped a lot. I was glad to be with Kris because so often, I found myself sad. But with her, I was able to enjoy our little place. This was the freedom that we'd been waiting for. And we did what any normal young adults would do. We partied all the time, had lots of company at our place, since we couldn't go out all that much because we had the kids. But it was a good time.

There was only one thing, though, that stands out in my mind about that time with Kris and it wasn't something good. One day while the kids were at school, I was at my mom's house, sitting on the porch and this guy that I knew who hung out with me and Kris and all of our other friends at our place sometimes, walked up and said, "Hey Shawnda, I left something over at your house."

I said, "You can go on over there. Kris is home."

"Nah, I just left from over there and she's not."

I didn't feel like doing it, but since I wasn't really doing anything, I went upstairs, grabbed my keys and we walked over to my place together.

When we got there, we entered the apartment. I closed the door behind us, and then told him I'd go get his stuff.

But when I came back out to the front room, he grabbed me, pulled me to him and started kissing me. At first, I was shocked and then, I started screaming, trying to push him away. He covered my mouth with his hands and knocked me to the floor. Then, before I could get up, he jumped on top of me.

He was too strong for me. No matter how much I punched, I couldn't get him off of me. He unbuttoned, then unzipped my pants. The only thing I could use was my feet and I started banging my heels against the floor. I hoped somebody, anybody would hear me. But no matter how much I kicked, he kept trying to take off my pants.

I struggled for so long that I became tired. There was nothing I could do—he was going to rape me. So, I calmed down and just laid there; I was so afraid of what he was going to do.

But then, someone knocked on the door. For a moment, he froze. When someone knocked again, he glared at me. "You better act normal," he said before he took his hand away from my mouth.

I was so relieved when he got up off of me. I got up, buttoned my pants and then opened the door. I was shaky when I saw my neighbor. She peeked into the apartment.

She said, "Are you okay?"

"Yeah," I said, trying to act normal like he told me to do.

She frowned a little like she really didn't believe me. "I heard a lot of banging up here." She stepped into the apartment without me asking her inside. She glanced at me and then, she looked at him.

She knew something was wrong because both of us just stood there quiet for a moment. Then, I said, "Yeah, it's cool. We were just leaving out." I waited, thinking that she was going to leave. But she didn't budge; she didn't move until I moved.

I said, "Okay," and then, I walked out the door and he followed me out. My neighbor was the last one to leave the apartment.

She stood next to me as I locked the door and she whispered to me, "You okay?"

I knew he was standing behind us, waiting to hear what I was going to say. "Yeah," I said.

I think it was only because we were outside the apartment that she said, "Okay." Then, she looked him up and down before she went back inside her place.

He was standing there, but my plan was that I was going to walk right by him and go back to my mother's house. But before I could get by him, he said, " You better never bring this up with anybody."

I just nodded.

"I'm not playing. You know what I'm capable of, so you know what would happen if you told anybody. You better keep your mouth shut."

All I did was walk around him without saying a word. But I didn't have to say anything; he knew that I would keep quiet. And he was right. I didn't say anything to anyone for decades. For years, there were only three people who knew about what almost happened that day and I am so grateful that my neighbor came down and saved me.

Chapter 21

And now, a new star was born. On October 19, 1992 I had another baby—a little boy that we nicknamed, Tay. I had to quit my job and now, I was back in my box. I couldn't believe it, but I wasn't the only one.

"What did you expect, Shawnda?" my mother said. "You have birth control pills, but you don't take them. This is what happens."

"I was taking them, but sometimes they made me so sick, I had to stop."

"You should have told your doctor. She could have changed the prescription. You should have been more responsible with this."

My mom was right, I wasn't responsible, but I had the cutest little boy. He had the biggest brown eyes you ever wanted to see. Just looking at him helped me adjust to this new life of once again being home all day and taking care of three kids. I really did want to get back to my career, but it would have to wait until Tay was at least one.

I did have a little bit of relief—Booney was in preschool now. I couldn't believe it and right away I saw an improvement in my son. He began speaking so much better, I guessed being around other kids helped him out a lot.

Things were good with me...well at least, they were good in terms of me not having to deal with money problems. Between my mother, my food stamps and the cash I was getting every month, my kids had everything they needed. So things should have been good for me—but they weren't. Mentally, I was off, always staring into space, daydreaming, wondering what my next step in life was going to be. I was only twenty-two years old, but I had three children. I began thinking that I would be a little more free in one year when Toota would be in school, and then, I would only have one child at home. At least I did have a career under my belt, but I had to stop having kids and putting myself back at square one.

I did love all of my kids, though, and the first year of Tay's life moved pretty quickly with all of my attention on the three of them. Now that Toota and Booney were both in school, I only had to worry about Tay. My baby boy was different than his big brother and sister. He didn't cry as much as Booney did, though he was a lot more active. He got into everything, and I mean everything, including the toilet, the garbage and he would eat anything that was on the floor. I couldn't take my eyes off of him for not even a moment.

One thing about him, though, he loved his brother and sister. When it was time for me to go and pick up the older two, Tay was so excited. We'd walk to the school and Tay would break loose from me. But before he even saw Booney or Toota, he would stop and talk to other kids that he didn't even know. Then when he saw his brother and sister, he would run to them.

We were into a good routine. When we got home from school, I'd help Booney and Toota with their homework and by the time we finished, Dell would have had their food ready for them to eat. After that, while they watched TV and played, Dell would get their clothes ready for the next day, while I did Toota's hair. It was such a blessing for me to have the help, especially from my brother, Dell. He was always there for me.

For years, that was my routine. I wasn't doing anything but taking care of the kids. I wasn't challenging myself mentally in any way. But I knew there was something going on with me. Inside, I wasn't happy. I just didn't have a name for it. I didn't know, that I was suffering from depression.

❧

Finally, it was time for Tay to go to school. He was so happy to be going, but so was I. I would have all three in school, even if it was only for half a day. But after he was in school for just a few weeks, I got a call from Tay's teacher.

"Shawnda, did you pick up your son?" Mrs. Davis asked me.

"No," I said with a frown. "Not yet. I'm on my way."

"Well, he's not in class."

"What?" I exclaimed. Oh, my God. There were only two people on the list to pick him up—me and Iris—and it wasn't even time to get him from school. "I'm on my way," I told his teacher.

I grabbed my stuff and ran out of my house, my heart was beating hard the whole time. Where was my son? Who had taken my son? The questions filled my head.

And then, when I was just a few blocks from the school, I saw this little boy coming toward me wearing a white turtleneck, brown pants and Air Ones...and of course, that big ass smile on his face.

"How the hell did you get out of school?" I screamed; I was so mad at him.

"I snuck out," he said, still smiling as if what he'd done was no big deal.

I was so happy to see him, but I was still so pissed, and still so scared. Something could have happened to him. I picked him up and hugged him, I was just so happy that he was safe. But I was still pissed and told him, "If you ever leave that school again by yourself, I'm gonna beat your ass, do you hear me?"

He nodded, but I was sure that he was confused with the way I was yelling and hugging him at the same time. He said, "So are we gonna go back to the school to pick up Booney and Toota?"

"No, they don't get out till 3:15, you know that."

I held his hand all the way home. When we got there, I called his teacher to let her know that I had him, then, he ate, changed his clothes and I helped him with his letters and numbers. This was something that I could be proud of. All three of my children were pretty smart. I never had any challenges with Booney and Toota, they always listened in school and did their work. And Tay loved to learn, too.

As the years went by, my kids continued doing well in school. I was so proud of all of them, but Tay started giving me problems. While he was smart, he was always disruptive in class and he was just in kindergarten. I just hoped that he was going to get better.

But he didn't get better at all.

Chapter 22

On May 14, 1997, I had another baby and my daughter, Tania was so different from the beginning. Tania was quiet from the start; even when she came out of my womb, she wasn't crying. The doctor was concerned at first, but all of her vitals were fine. The doctor had to make her cry and she only cried a little.

Everyone was so excited; the kids rushed home to see her. Toota was so happy to have a little sister.

Now, I was the mother of four kids and even if I had wanted to work, I didn't know how I would do it. It was hard to find a babysitter with four kids, but my sister and I made a deal. She would watch my kids and then, I'd pay her. But that only lasted a few months before my sister quit...and it was because of Tay.

Tay was getting worse, always so bad. We got so many calls from the school, that we took turns going up there for him and he was too bad for even my sister.

"He's hard-headed," my sister told me. "He's too bad."

So once again, I had to turn to my mom and Dell who helped out, but it was hard. As the years went by, Tay got worse and by the time he was in the third grade, he was getting suspended for fighting. Almost every day I got a call from Guggenheim Elementary (the same place where I went to school and fought all the time) about Tay and his fighting.

I was always up at the school and I remembered how my mother always had to be at the school because of me. It was constant. But then, a change came to my life. My Section 8 housing came through and I was so happy about it. I wasn't the only one; shit, my mom's eyes lit up when she heard that I was taking my kids and moving into my own place. She was filled with joy!

I found a place on Laflin, a three bedroom, single family house. It was good to have my own space, but my life changed in another way, too—I wasn't able to keep my job. I wanted to work, but I spent so much time up at the school because of Tay, that I had to stay home. Tay would get suspended and then, when he returned to school, he would be there for a few days before he was suspended again!

I told Tay that I was done. I wasn't going up to the school anymore and I meant that. Well, my son found a way around that. He got one of the guys, who hung out on the next block over, to go up to the school for him. I don't know how he convinced him, but I only found out about it when I ran into the guy at the corner store and he told me everything. All I could say to him was thank you.

One of the times when I had to go to the school to get Tay, we were walking home when I heard a horn blowing behind me. I was so busy lecturing Tay, that I didn't pay attention. But the horn kept blowing and blowing and finally, I looked at the white truck and my face lit up.

It was my Rambo!

He stuck his head out the window and hollered, "You still live there?"

"Yeah," I grinned.

He waved, then he kept going. I wished that he would turn around and come back, but he didn't. But just seeing him even for that little while was good enough for me. I hadn't seen Rambo since high school and it was just good to see his face.

I wondered about Rambo because my life had changed so much. I wasn't that skinny high school freshman anymore. I was a mother with four kids, living on my own. I had my own place, but I really didn't like it and we didn't stay there that much. There was nothing wrong with my place. It was just that when we were there, it was just me and the kids. I was used to having my mama around. I guessed that 7220 would always be the place I called home.

But one thing that was good about being in my own place was that my friend, Yvonne, was just a block away. Yvonne had grown up with my sister, Mia and she had been close to our family for so many years, always looking out for me like a sister. When the kids were at school, sometimes, I would go over and sit with her and whenever she could, she helped me and the kids out. She would keep an eye on Tay for me whenever he was hanging out on her block. And she fed us anytime she cooked.

It was good because her kids were about the same age as mine and they were friends, hanging out and going to school together. They looked out for each other and Yvonne looked out for them, the same way she used to look out for me.

Yvonne really looked out for Tay, but she wasn't the only one. Any time Tay did something wrong, someone would be knocking on my door telling me, "Tay did this," or "Tay did that." And the problems with my son, just kept escalating.

The worst time was when a neighbor knocked on my door. I'd opened it quickly because it was late and Tay wasn't home. But there was a man standing there, holding onto Tay by his shirt collar.

"Is this yours?" my neighbor asked me, holding up a gun.

My mouth and eyes opened wide. "Oh, my God. Yes," I said taking my gun away from him.

He said, "Well, your son had it, trying to stick up Harold's Chicken. I caught him, snatched his ass up and brought him home. He could have hurt someone and himself."I couldn't believe this. I had hidden my gun in a safe place, but I guessed it wasn't hidden enough for Tay. When that man left, I asked my son, "What were you thinking? Are you crazy?"

Before he could even answer, I tried to knock Tay's soul out of his nine-year-old body and when I was done, I told him that he better come straight home from school every day, and not to have his friends knocking on my door.

I found a new place for my gun, hoping this time, no one would find it. And I kept my eye on Tay. He listened to me for about a week, but then, he went right back to his old ways and not coming straight home. I did everything I possibly could to get control of him, but nothing worked.

That was when I knew I had to go back to 7220. I needed help with these kids and my mother and especially, Dell, would be able to help me.

My plan was to leave my house in another week or two, but one morning, I got a call from Mia. It was early, the kids weren't even up yet.

"Shawnda, you've got to come over here right now," she said.

"Why? What's wrong?"

"It's Dell, something's wrong with him."

"Okay."

So, I got the kids up and got ready to go to my mother's house. It was so hot that day, I wanted to take the bus. But I was broke as usual, so we had to walk the ten or so blocks as fast as we could.

When we got to the house, it was filled with people and I could tell by the look on everyone's faces, something was very wrong.

Mia came out and cried, "He's gone, Shawnda."

"What?"

"Dell is gone."

My tears were instant. I started crying and couldn't stop. My big brother, Dell had died? I was outdone, speechless, all of that. He was the person who loved me and my kids the most; I didn't know what I was going to do.

I wasn't the only one who was upset, though. My kids loved their uncle and they were hurt. But Tania seemed to be hurt the most. She had gotten quiet and was lethargic. I was so concerned that I took her to the E.R. The doctors discovered that she was dehydrated to the bone, and I realized that the walk over in the hot sun had probably done that to her.

"We're going to have to put her on an IV," the doctor told me. "And we're going to have to keep her overnight."

I couldn't believe that this was happening. First Dell, and now, my baby. But then, while we were waiting for the doctors to run tests on her, I noticed something—Tania wasn't talking.

"Are you okay?" I asked her.

She nodded.

I asked her a few more questions and all she would do was shake or nod her head. She wouldn't talk at all. Now, I was really worried that something was seriously wrong. The doctors performed all kinds of tests on her—urine and blood tests, but all of her lab work came back fine.

She was kept overnight and then the next day, my sisters went to the hospital with me, and all of us tried to get Tania to talk. But she wouldn't say a word. It was like the death of her uncle had taken her speech away.

She was released from the hospital in two days.

I was glad when she was home, but we were all suffering. After Dell passed away, I had to just stay in my house on Laflin. I couldn't stay in 7220. There were too many memories there.

My brother's death sent me into a real slump and as the days went by, it didn't get better. I stayed in bed most of the time, leaving my oldest children to take care of Tania and make sure that she ate. I was slipping deeper and deeper down and I had no idea how to get out of it.

My mother was going through a lot. First Dell died, and then a year later, my other brother, Marcellus and then, my grandmother died. Three straight years, three deaths. It just seemed that month after month, year after year something bad was happening to our family. And no matter what, there was nothing that I could do about it. After all that my mom had done for me, I wanted to help her through these difficult emotional times.

But how could I help her when I couldn't even help myself? I certainly hadn't helped my kids. I was supposed to be grown now, but I was only grown in age, not mentally. I was still acting young, going from job to job, not saving money, being materialistic buying my kids gym shoes and clothes rather than spending the time instilling in them the kinds of things that my mother had been instilling in me my whole life.

I wasn't passing on what I learned and it showed. Three of my kids were good—Booney, Toota and Tania, but that Tay—he was my biggest challenge.

There were times when I just wanted to stay in bed with the covers over my head and just feel sorry for myself. I was tired of being a lazy bum. And I knew within me that I could do better, much, much better.

Chapter 23

Tay was a difficult child. That was all that I could say. He was so bad that he couldn't go to family birthday parties or get togethers because no one wanted to be bothered with him. He was out of control and I didn't know what to do.

It was like Tay just had his own mind and he was going to do what he wanted to do. It was bad though. He wouldn't act right in school, he was disrespectful to adults. I knew this was all my fault; I should have started from the beginning with him. But I did a lot of lecturing, not enough whooping.

I began to realize that maybe I was failing my children as a parent. I taught them how to brush their teeth, comb their hair, how to take a bath every day, and always wear clean clothes. But I didn't teach them about every day life and the consequences that come when you don't do the right thing.

I tried to make up for some of it by getting Tay involved in things he liked. Like Booney, he loved basketball. So when he was in the fifth grade, we signed him up for the basketball team and for a while, that kept Tay happy and focused.

But he couldn't stay on the team because his grades were bad. When he was taken off the team, he acted like he didn't care. "I'll just play on the playground after school," he told me.

That broke my heart. It was like my son just didn't care. I remember how I didn't care about school, but I wanted more for my children.

Everyone kept telling me that Tay just needed a man in his life. I wasn't sure if that was true. Dell had been there for him and I knew plenty of single women who had raised wonderful children. Brenda, the mother of my brother's daughter was only fourteen when she got pregnant. But she took on the responsibility seriously. She did what she had to do: cooked, cleaned, worked... and she raised her daughter well. Having a child so young didn't keep her down and she raised my niece to do so well. My niece went to school, college, then she went on to get her MBA from DePaul University.

And Yvonne was the same way. She raised five kids on her own, and every single one of her children are very respectful and were all doing well in school.

So I guessed it was just different for every person. Maybe there were some kids that really did need a father figure and it seemed that my son, Tay, was that boy that needed a real man.

Part 2
Booney

Chapter 24

Raising Booney was easy. He was a quiet boy, not talking till he was about three. I'd taken him to a doctor when I realized he wasn't trying to talk by the time he was two. The doctor asked me about my environment at home, and with all of my siblings there in the house, she felt that we could work with him.

"Don't speak to him in baby talk," the doctor told me.

That was something that we did all the time. Once we stopped that, Booney improved and then got much better when he went to school. I guess being around other kids really helped and my son, who would never talk before, started talking his ass off.

While he was a sweet little guy most of the time, he could also be mean because he had a temper. But there was one thing about Booney—he enjoyed school. He was on point all the way from Pre-K, through kindergarten, and grammar school. He really did well. Not only was he doing well with his classes, but he enjoyed sports and because he was so tall and quick, he loved basketball and I was glad when he played on the Guggenheim team.

Booney was doing so well that when he failed the 7th grade, we were all shocked. My son was so angry about that and so was I. It wasn't about his grades, it was the tests that were the problem for him. Booney was never good at taking tests and when he failed, I transferred him to another school, thinking that would help him. I ended up transferring him three times, but all of his teachers told me that same thing.

"Booney is a good student, but taking tests is his weakness."

It was my mom who told me that I couldn't keep moving Booney around like that. She said he had to get settled somewhere, so within that year, I ended up sending him back to Guggenheim.

My mother had been right. Booney was able to turn it around then, and he did so much better on his test-taking after he joined some after-school programs that tutored him and helped him a lot.

Booney was always well liked by lots of kids. He had so many friends but he also got into a lot of fights which had him suspended a couple of times. It wasn't that he was a fighter, like me. Booney just had a temper, and when he got mad, that was it. Even though he was always respectful, he would even talk back to his teachers if he felt he wasn't being respected or he was angry. But that didn't happen too often because overall, he was a good kid who loved fashion and loved money.

I was protective of my oldest child, wanting to shelter him. When he was younger, he did everything I asked. He come straight home from school and when he was out, I knew where he was at all times. As he aged, he began hanging out and I began to worry.

"Always come home before dark," I told him all the time. "There's too much going on in the streets."

But Booney feared nothing and no one. He was hanging out on Green Street with a lot of these older guys. It wasn't all bad, though. Those guys over there knew all the kids. Everyone knew who each kid belonged to, so the older guys looked out for the younger ones and I knew he was pretty safe over there.

There was no way for me to keep Booney away from those guys anyway. My son had such a thirst for knowledge. That was what drew him to the older guys, he wanted a kind of knowledge that I couldn't give him, so I had to let him be since his father wasn't around.

I was proud of him, though, really proud and when he was graduating from 8th grade, to me, that was his time to shine. He'd done so well in school that I got him everything he wanted. How could I not do that? He'd passed all of his classes, and at his graduation luncheon, he won a couple of awards.

It was all so exciting. I was ready for him to go to high school. But before he would enter the 9th grade, he had to first get through the summer. The summer with Booney was tough. He would play his XBox and basketball, but he got bored so easily; it was difficult for me to keep him from getting distracted and when he got distracted, he would hang out on the streets and shoot dice.

I was so glad when summer was over and Booney was happy, too. There was no doubt that he would do well in high school. He'd been eager to go, just like me all those years ago. My son always thought ahead and planned for his future and he had plans of what he wanted to do at Dunbar.

I did my best to prepare him for high school. "You're going to meet a lot of different people there," I told him. "Some will like you and some won't, but don't you worry about none of that. What's important is that you stay focused, you keep a leveled-head and you stay confident. But always remember to have fun and just enjoy. These are the best days of your life."

I told him all the things that I expected from high school, and then even the kinds of things that had scared me.

"That school is big," I said, remembering my first day at Robeson. "It's way different than Guggenheim. There are going to be six or seven hundred students there."

I hoped that Booney was listening to me better than I had listened to my mother. I told him about being his own person and making his own choices, never letting anyone lead him into something he didn't want to do. I told him to choose his own path and to do it for himself and for no one else.

It sounded like he was listening to me, but he always said, "I know, Ma, I know."

Booney knew everything if you let him tell it. But I did feel as if he was ready for what was in front of him because he'd been thinking about high school for a long time.

"I want to try out for basketball and football," he told me.

I liked that idea because I wanted him to be well rounded in school and do more than just take classes. At his orientation, we inquired about all the sports teams and were given the information we needed. Then we got his class schedule and I was surprised for a moment. I hoped he was ready for this because he would have some long days—from first period to tenth period. My son didn't quite understand what all of that meant, but I explained to him all the things I hadn't known...how he was going to move from one class to the other, how sometimes, it could not only be confusing, but overwhelming.

But the most important thing I'd try to give to him was something that my mother had told me. "If you pay attention in class from the beginning, the ending will go very well for you. You won't have to be playing catch up in your classes. That's the best way to stay on top of everything. And you're going to have to stay on top of everything because I won't be able to help you with your homework, especially not anything that has to do with that damn math."

He laughed. "Why won't you be able to help me with my homework?"

"I only have an eighth grade education."

That surprised my son. "You dropped out of school? Why? What happened?"

This was the first time that we talked about this and I was happy to tell Booney what happened to me, hoping that my story would be a good lesson for him. "I made some bad choices for myself. I'm not making any excuses for how my life turned out. It's my own fault."

"Did you drop out because you had kids?"

"No, of course not. Having kids should have motivated me more to do better. But it didn't. I had the same opportunity as everyone else. That's why I'm always saying to you not to be like your mama. You're really smart and I don't want you to struggle the way I have and end up with nothing. Just focus on your work, getting out of high school and becoming a real man so that you won't have to live off of anyone, you won't have to wait for a handout, you won't have to borrow or get money from anyone."

"Okay, Ma. I got this."

"I'm serious," I told him. "I want you to do well so that you will have your own money, your own house, your own car. I want you to have a career that you love and can be proud of."

"I will, Ma. I told you, I got this. We gonna be rich and I'm going to take care of you. We're gonna be living good."

I smiled. "Okay," I said. Booney had big dreams, and even though I didn't know what he planned to do, I knew for a fact that he could achieve anything he put his mind to. He was capable of having it all. And I felt like he deserved it.

I only hoped that my son was really listening to me and taking my advice, which was something that I never did and still regretted. But I had faith that he would do well. I paid his school fees so that everything would be in place on his first day. Then, I went shopping and bought three or four outfits and of course, some new black and white Air Ones so he'd be set for school. I didn't feel like it was enough, though. Even though I had a good job working in a pediatric office, I had the expense of taking care of four children and all of my household bills. While I wasn't able to give Booney everything he wanted, I was able to give him what he needed. I think being the oldest and having to live with that made him stronger and made him work hard for what he wanted.

Booney was ready, and I was excited he was starting this next chapter of his life, but when the time really came for him to go to high school I wasn't ready. I was scared about so many things, but the biggest thing was the bus route. Not only was it a long ride since we lived farther from the school, but he would have to stand and wait for the bus every morning. All I hoped was that no one would bother him or try to bully him and trigger him to begin to run his mouth. Yes, he could defend himself, but that was part of the problem. I was concerned about his temper.

"When you get on that bus, make sure you pay attention so that you won't get lost."

"Okay, Ma. I'll be fine."

But even though he said that, on the first day of school, I wanted to go with him.

"Really?" Booney laughed when I told him that.

He may have thought that was funny, but I really was scared for him, so much so, that I was crying on the inside. I knew I was going overboard with everything but it felt like I was letting go of my first born, my oldest son. I always worried, always had a fear of him being on his own. It would just continue to get worse as he got older.

It turned out that Booney was just fine his first year in high school, as I should have known that he would be. Every day, I made sure he had his pack of bus cards and lunch money and that was all that I had to worry about. I never had to wake him up for school, he got up early every day and went to class. I never had to check on his homework, which was a good thing because that was one of the reasons I told him to pay attention in class.

He knew what to do, and he just did it without any fuss or any complaints. He was a go-getter like that and that would be a good characteristic for him to have in his life.

Booney's first year rolled along. Like always, his grades were good because he loved school. He was doing well in his classes, and he was on the football team. I was happy he'd made new friends. Booney was popular and knew a lot of people. But there were three guys that he truly called his friends, Chino, SB and Rell.

My son was growing in front of my eyes. He was getting so tall, he was 6'2" now, and so of course, he bugged me for new clothes because he was even more into fashion now that he was in high school. But he had to survive off of three new outfits with every one of my pay periods.

It was in his sophomore year when things began to shift for Booney. He began to slack off and his priorities changed. Now, he was more into hanging out and going to parties. He was doing things that I wasn't used to. It felt like he was breaking away from the shelter that I'd tried to give him. That shelter was coming to an end, though. He was growing up.

He even lost interest in football. He'd made the team again, but he didn't want to stay on it. The coach wanted me to encourage him to continue playing, but there was nothing I could do. After just a couple of practices, Booney said the practice was too hard, too strenuous for him. So he quit, and turned in his football equipment and was done!

But Booney still loved to watch football and basketball games on television. He could watch all day. At first, I thought it was just because he enjoyed the game, but I would soon find out that it may have been more than that.

Chapter 25

For a while, Booney had loved shooting dice. But soon, it became a bad habit, almost an obsession. He began shooting dice for money, using what I gave him for spending. I didn't find out about this until he got into a fight with one of his older cousins and my sister told me what he was doing.

I was mad when I found out how he was gambling and how he was spending money on that. "I'm not giving you anymore money."

"No, Ma. It was just this one time."

Did he really think I believed that? Did he really think I was slow like that? He still asked for money, though his favorite reason was, "I'm going to buy some Harold's Chicken."

If he was hungry, I had to give him money. I would reach in my purse and give him ten dollars.

He would look at that money like, 'What is this?' and, I would stare right back at him and say, "Nigga, give it back to me, then."

"You don't have a twenty?"

"No, and if that ten isn't enough for you, then you better go eat what granny cooked for you."

He'd take that ten dollar bill with his slick ass. My son was all about the money. He knew my pay period better than I did. He'd call me at work and tell me to cash my check before I got home 'cause he needed some new Air Ones and an outfit, a pair of Girbaud jeans and a shirt.

But even though I'd caught my son that time, Booney was still gambling like a grown person. He'd gone from just playing dice to betting on basketball games. When he lost money, I had to pay the difference because I knew what it was like out there and what would happen to him if he owed someone money.

"These people will hurt you about their money. You need to stop betting because I won't always have it for you to give to them. Then what will you do? Just stop it."

But the way my mother used to lecture me and I didn't listen, now my words were going in one of my son's ears and out the other.It came to a head one night when Booney was with his cousin at a park in Markham shooting dice when the police rolled up on them. Unfortunately, this was something that always happened to young men in Chicago, but this time the police gave them a break. They weren't supposed to be shooting dice, so the cops broke them all up, and told them to leave.

Booney, his cousin and the other guys pretended to be leaving the park, but when the officers drove away, those boys went right back to shooting dice. Well, the police weren't stupid. They circled back around and caught them. Now, I don't know if Booney was winning or losing, but he got so upset that the police were breaking up the game, that he started cussing the cops out. There was no way the police were going to be disrespected that way. So, they went to handcuff Booney and he resisted arrest. They tussled with him, trying to get him in the car. It took another car to come to help them before they got Booney into the back seat.

I was sitting at home, watching TV when Booney's cousin called and began to explain the situation to me.

"He fought two or three cops. It took them a while, but they finally handcuffed him and put Booney in the car. They're gonna lock him up."

I got off that phone and dashed down to the police station. I couldn't believe it. My fifteen-year-old son was in jail! At first,

I was worried, but when I got there, my worry turned to anger. From the moment I walked in the door, I could hear Booney cussing like crazy.

I checked in at the front desk and when the officer realized who I was, he looked at me and said, "Do you hear your son?"

All I could do was shake my head. When they brought Booney out to me, I would have thought that he would calm down. But he got worse.

"Ma, these are some bitch ass niggas," he shouted. "They took my money and...." He went on and on and on.

"Booney, you need to calm down," I kept telling him. I wanted to hear his side of the story, but while I was standing right there, he was going back and forth with the police.

"Ma, his bitch ass is mad 'cause I slammed him."

Now, I was really pissed. Didn't Booney understand that messing with the police that way could have gotten him killed? I tried to stop him over and over until I finally said, "Shut the fuck up before I leave your ass in here."

That got my son to shut his mouth. He didn't speak anymore then, and he was quiet the entire ride home. I let him go on to bed that night, but the next day, I still had something to say.

"That police station has a bad reputation," I said. "You putting your hands on an officer is the most disrespectful thing you've ever done. You could have been killed, or brutally hurt. When they told you to leave, your ass should have left the park, period. No if, ands or buts about it. When a police officer tells you to do something, you do it. That's it. "

"But you should hear how they were talking to me," Booney said.

"It doesn't matter. This whole thing wouldn't have escalated if you would have listened to them the first time they told you to leave the park."

All Booney did was shake his head and that reminded me of what I would do when my mother tried to talk to me.

But still, I kept trying to talk to him. "You know I won't tell you nothing wrong. You need to learn to listen to me and get past your anger. You'll be fine if you can just learn to do that."

I wasn't sure if Booney really heard me, but I hoped that he did. He was this mixture of a well-mannered, respectful kid with the worst temper ever. What a combination and I just hoped that didn't lead to trouble.

But I had one more thing to tell his ass before this was over for me. "Don't you ever disrespect me like that with all of that cussing."

He acted like he was surprised that I'd said that. "I never cuss in front of you."

I was almost speechless. "Are you serious? You were cursing your ass off at the police station."

He looked at me as if he almost didn't believe me. "Really?"

My son really didn't remember, that's how mad he got when he was triggered. I was just happy that his anger didn't get him more than just locked up...at least not this time. But the problem was, it didn't end there.

My son had made it through freshman year, sophomore year, junior year and he waited until his senior year to act a plum fool.

First, Mr. Three-the-Hard-Way was going to jail for what the school called mob action. A whole bunch of kids got into a big fight right outside of school and the police were called. I couldn't believe it. It was total chaos, on the news and everything. I had to go down to the police station and get Booney and his friends out of there.

But that didn't stop the trouble that Booney was getting into. He and his friends were getting into mob action with the kids from the nearby Phillips High School. It was just terrible; they were fighting all the time. They almost didn't make it to prom. In order for Booney to go, I had to go up to the school, talk to the principal and then Booney and I had to take a parenting class together.

He was able to go to prom and I was so glad about that because this was the end of his high school career. He had a turquoise and white suit tailor-made and the only thing he didn't like was that he couldn't wear sneakers, he had to wear white dress shoes. He was so upset about that because he wore sneakers everywhere.

"Boy, this is your prom. Your shoes are minor," I told him.

But he carried his One's with him, so he would be able to change into them at some point.

Before graduation, I had to take care of a couple of school fees totaling about $500 for Booney. That covered things like lost books, temporary IDs and other expenses I hadn't paid for. But finally graduation was here and I was so proud of Booney. He was about to graduate from high school, something that I hadn't done. For his graduation, I wanted to give him whatever he wanted because to me, graduating from high school was a big accomplishment. He deserved this and I had started saving my money for this occasion at the beginning of his senior year.

And then, graduation day came...and I was so sad.

My heart was broken because Tay's graduation from 8th grade and Booney's graduation from high school were the same day. I explained to Tay that while both graduations were important, I had to go to Booney's because this was for high school. My heart was so hurt, but Tay understood. I had my friend, Yvonne, to attend his graduation and take plenty of pictures.

What I was able to do was to get everyone together at the house, the morning of the graduations and everyone in the family was there. We took pictures and then, we headed out to the graduation. As I sat in the audience with the hundreds of other parents, siblings, aunts, uncles and friends, I was so proud. My baby had made it through high school just like he told me he would.

Booney already had plans after graduation. He wanted to go to college, but he wanted to take a year off first. I tried to encourage him to go straight to college because I was afraid that if he took one year off, it would become two, then three and then, he would never go.

But Booney insisted that he just wanted a little time off and he had it all planned out. He, along with Chino and SB had decided to move to Iowa to work at a Tyson's factory. They had applied and gotten the jobs after they graduated. I was proud that Booney was taking care of business. I was really happy about that, but sad at the same time when they left for Iowa just a few months later.

They didn't have to do a lot of planning when it came to where they were going to live. They knew someone in Iowa and they were just going to move in with him and then all four of them would split the rent.

When he was gone, I had to sit back for a moment and really think about what I'd accomplished. My first born was a high school graduate and living on his own. We both had done something right.

Chapter 26

Booney was out there and doing it. He was making good money in Iowa and I didn't have to worry about him. He didn't have time to run the streets; he didn't have time to do anything, he was working twelve hours a day. So in between work, that only left time for him to eat and sleep.

One thing that was good about him working all of those hours was that Booney saved all of his money. Well, not all of his money—he was still into clothes, so he shopped and shopped, but he was able to put a good deal of the money away since he worked so many hours.

After he had been in Iowa for six months, he decided that he really did want to go to college and I was excited about that.

But after just a few weeks of research, Booney decided not to go to college at all because it was so expensive. I told him that there were grants and loans he could get for school, but even though I wanted him to go to college, I left it alone. Booney was really a young man now and although I could give him advice, he had to make his own decisions.

All of them did decide to come back home, though. And now, they had a new job; they became the managers for Smurkio.

Now, they didn't know anything about being managers, but what they had going for them, was that they were willing to work hard, recording in the studio and promoting. While I didn't think anything was going to come of this, they proved me wrong. They were getting it done, taking care of business.

Often, they held meetings at our house, putting their heads together, trying to figure out all the ways they could make Smurkio a star. Those times were hectic because they were all so different. They would voice their opinions and the discussion would be all over the place. They were trying to decide all kinds of things: what video to do, what song should be first, who should do what.

The meetings would be long, sometimes it felt like an eight-hour workday and when I was off on Saturdays, I didn't feel like having all of that going on in my house.

But like I said, they worked so hard creating buzz for Smurkio and it began to pay off. They began to make money, which was cool. Smurkio was doing shows and features on other rapper's songs. They had him doing lots of interviews and he was gaining a lot of popularity on YouTube and his rap videos. The only problem was, the more money they made, the more problems that came with it.

I was a nervous wreck. Now, I was always a worry-bug about my boys. It was hard on me when they stayed out late or were away from home for long periods of time. There were times when I wouldn't hear from them for a week and that was hard for me as a mother when I was used to seeing their faces and speaking to them every day.

But it seemed the more successful they became, the less I saw them. They were losing sight of everything except the money. The money was blinding them—that was all they could see.

They loved giving me money and I know they felt that was one way they were taking care of me. But that money didn't mean anything to me. I wanted to see and hear from them. Fuck the money.

It didn't help that more and more people were in their circle. Their circle got so big that whenever people came over to our house, I had to ask Booney, "Who is this?"

"Oh, Ma, that's just one of the guys."

But I had to ask that question so many times, that I finally had to tell Booney to stop letting so many people into our house. "If it ain't SB, Chino, or Rell, don't bring them here."

The stress of what he was doing was getting to me. My hair was coming out, my blood pressure was rising—hell, I didn't even know I had high blood pressure until then. But I found that out the hard way.

But I had to admit that they were becoming successful. There were more YouTube views, more appearances and interviews, and Smurk's popularity just continued to grow. The money was coming in fast. They were meeting and greeting and bumping heads with so many people.

One day, he asked if he could take my Nina with him.

I said, "No, where's yours?"

He said, "I left it at Granny's."

"Okay, but bring it right back."

Later on that day, when I was just sitting watching TV, I received a call from one of Booney's friends.

"Booney's been shot," was all he said.

I literally shitted on myself. I didn't know where, I didn't know how hurt he was or anything. I told my daughter, Tania and then, I was shaking as I jumped in the shower (I had to) and then got dressed. Tania and I rushed to the hospital to find out about my baby.

When I got to the hospital and was taken to Booney's room, I busted out crying as soon as I saw my baby. Even though he was sitting up in the bed and talking and I could tell that he was going to be fine, I couldn't stop crying. I was just so grateful that he was alive because I'd been so scared.

Booney kept saying, "Ma, you've got to stop crying."

But then when they told me that he was being transferred to another hospital for surgery, I cried some more—even when they said he'd be fine.

"I'm okay, Ma. You've got to stop crying."

"Don't tell me that...these are tears of joy and I'm thanking God that you're going to be okay."

When we were alone in the room, Booney told me, "Ma, if I didn't take her with me, I don't know what the outcome would have been."

"Then, I'm glad I let you take her with you."

"Me too because you usually don't."

While he was taken to the other hospital by ambulance, I followed in my car. He had surgery that night and the following day, I didn't leave my baby's side.

After his three-day stay in the hospital, he came home, and I sat him down. We were about to have a long talk because there was a lot going on that I had let pass. He didn't know, but I knew everything. When he was out in the streets, if anything happened, I knew.

If he got arrested, he told everyone, "Don't tell my mama," but I knew.

If he got into it with someone, he told everyone, "Don't tell my mama," but I knew.

If anything went down, he told everyone, "Don't tell my mama," but like I said, I knew everything and I had to put a stop to what was going on.

Before I even began my lecture, Booney said, "Ma, you're going to give me a headache."

I guess he didn't like my lectures anymore than I liked the lectures that my mother used to give to me. But the thing was I had been making bad decisions, but the decisions I was making back in the day wasn't life and death. Booney was living on the edge and I didn't care what he said, he was going to listen to me.

"If you don't want a headache, then make different moves, make smarter moves." I talked to Booney about how he had to move different in the streets. "If you make a bad decision, it doesn't just affect you. Your whole family from me to your sisters, your aunts, your uncles, your granny...everyone would be affected if anything happened to you. It would be a trickling affect and you have to think about that."

I kept talking to him, but all I could do was hope that he heard me.

Chapter 27

My talking to Booney didn't help much because the next year, he got shot again. This time, it was Tay who called me. From the moment I heard my son's voice, I knew something was wrong.

"Ma, where you at?" Tay asked.

I frowned. "I'm home."

"Okay, Ma. He got shot."

"Who got shot?"

"D-Thang."

"Who the fuck is D-Thang?"

When he said, "Booney," I sat straight up. "What the fuck?" I started screaming, "Is he okay? Is he okay?"

"Ma, calm down. I talked to him so he's good." Tay told me what hospital they were at and once again Tania and I rushed to the hospital. All I wanted to do was talk to the doctor.

Everyone kept saying that he was okay, he was okay. But he couldn't have been okay. No one was okay if they kept getting shot. It was just too much.

This time, Booney didn't need surgery because all of the bullets went in and he had exit wounds. After the doctors ran tests, the police came to talk to Booney, but my son didn't have anything to say to them. He told them he didn't know anything and that was it. They tried, but they finally left.

I was told that he would only be there for a few hours, so once I knew that he was going to be all right, I was ready to leave. I wasn't feeling well, but it was more than physically. I was hurt, I was numb, I was speechless, scared, confused and angry. He was only in there for a few hours before he was released.

So, I told him that I was going home. "I'll see you tomorrow," I said. "I love you."

"I love you, too, Ma."

I went home still filled with all of those emotions. This was a lot for me to handle.

The next day, I put in for Booney's prescriptions, then took the medication to him. And the moment I walked into the door, I gave him a headache with one of my lectures. I didn't care. I didn't care about him getting a headache or being in any kind of pain. I had to tell him what I knew. If he stayed out there like that, this wasn't going to be good.

It didn't matter what I said because the next year...Booney got shot again. Even thinking about this now, I cannot believe it. This time, Booney being shot was the worst experience of my life.

The call came in at three in the morning and I was in California. A friend of mine, Nikki said, "Did you hear what happened to D-Thang?"

This time, I knew who he was talking about. My heart began beating fast. "No," I said.

"He got shot and the police had everything taped off like it was a major crime scene."

The moment I hung up, I was so sick. I had to run to the bathroom and throw up, but that didn't help much. I felt dizzy, was having heart palpitations and I knew my blood pressure had shot up. I needed to relax so that I could get back to my son.

Tania was crying and trying to take care of me, but there was so much confusion. My phone was blowing up, but I didn't answer. I had to get back to Chicago and all I could do was pray that I could get on a flight. I called the airlines and luckily, there was room on the first flight at 7am.

Even though my phone kept ringing, I didn't answer except for two or three people. My flight was going to be long and I didn't want to hear anything else from anybody because I'd heard enough. It had been taped off like a crime scene—I knew that whatever happened to Booney was bad.

I was so grateful for Tania because my daughter really did try to take care of me and comfort me at the same time. When we got to the airport, I texted everyone who had been calling me, telling them that I didn't want to talk, I didn't want to hear anything until I got back to Chicago. I didn't care whether it was good or bad news, either way I'd see it for myself in three and a half hours.

When we got on the plane, all I could do was cry and pray. I just wanted to see my baby alive. The flight was the longest three and a half hours ever. It felt like three and a half days and I used that time to pray and so did Tania.

Like all the other times, when we hit the ground, I headed straight to the hospital. But once we were in the Uber, I wondered if we were ever going to get there. Not only was it a long ride from the airport, but the driver was driving so slow.

When we got to the hospital, I found out the truth. This time, it was bad. He had been shot several times all over his body. But he was alive and I thanked God for giving Booney another chance.

He was in a lot of pain and once again, he had to have surgery. There was no way I was going home, so I got a hotel room near the hospital. The next day, I was with my son from sun up to sun down but this time, he was so different from the last two times when he'd been shot.

Even though Booney had so many visitors, people coming in and out of his room, he was relatively quiet as if he was doing a lot of deep thinking. I left him alone for a little while to get him some clothes. He needed underwear and T-shirts. When I came back to his room and handed him the packages, he busted out laughing.

I didn't know what was so funny. He said, "Who's going to put these on?"

"What's wrong with those?"

"Fruit of the Looms?" He cracked up laughing.

"Shit, I didn't know what to get your ass."

I was just so happy to see him laugh. To me, that meant that he was getting better and I wanted it to stay that way. That's why I told him that he had too many people coming to visit him and he needed to cut it down. But I knew that wasn't going to happen. While I sat there in the hospital with him, I really wanted to talk and ask him so many questions, like: what happened, who did this?

I didn't ask him anything, though. More than the other times, he was really so hurt and heartbroken this time because it wasn't like all the others. This time, someone died and it was someone close—it was one of his cousins. So, I didn't question him. I just stayed quiet, knowing that my son would eventually talk to me.

But once he did, I knew he would never be the same.

I had to give him one of my headache lectures. "You've been shot all of these times and you're still here. You have a purpose for your life and you need to find out what it is." I hoped he really heard me, but I could see that he was done with me and what I was saying.

All he said after I finished was, "Ma, I'll see you tomorrow," and then, he said to Tania, "How do you put up with Ma's mouth? It never stops going, Man."

"Yeah, 'cause talking to your ass is like talking to a brick wall. So, I am ready to go."

But then, he said, "I hear you now, Ma. Everything you've been telling me, I hear it clear as day now. I'll see you tomorrow."

I kissed him and before I stepped out of the room, he said, "I love you, Ma."

"I love you, too, son."

❧

As a mother, I worried about all of my kids, but Booney was the one I worried about most. He was a good kid, and he's grown into a good man. His challenge is that he just doesn't listen. From the time he was younger, he just thought that he knew everything. So it was hard to lecture him because he hardly listened—just like me growing up.

But as he grew older, I began to see a big difference in Booney. He became a better listener and that made him smarter. He cut his circle down, which I knew would be a good thing for him. And the best part is that he became a great father. He loves his children, loves caring for them, loves teaching them, and he loves nurturing them so that they will group up into good adults. He is a bit stern, but other than that, to me, he is a one-of-a-kind dad who is adored by his children.

Life isn't all perfect, Booney and I still butt heads, but that's natural, I think. It doesn't happen often. What he does the most is to make sure I'm good at all times.

I always want Booney to know that he doesn't owe me anything. So, I give him one of my headache lectures, though I think he likes this one.

"Everything you got, you earned it. You worked hella hard for it and not only do you not owe me, you don't owe anyone. Everyone has a choice, just like you had. Everyone has a chance, just like you had. You chose the right path. So let no grown, healthy man or woman live off the fruit of your labor. It's good to help people, but don't stop their progress. You've done what you were supposed to do...now let them take their path."

Part 3
Tay

Chapter 28

I've called him this before, but it's true—Tay was a star on that day he was born in October 19, 1992. Now that I had two children, I promised myself that was it. Two was enough; I wasn't having anymore, especially since Tay was such a handful. I could tell he was going to be a lot when he was born. He cried so loud in the hospital and then, when I brought him home. But I became sure of how tough it was going to be with Tay on the day he snuck out of preschool and was about to walk home by himself. Tay always thought of himself as a big boy, even at the age of four. He thought he was grown and that was one thing that was never going to change about him.

Tay was always independent, but he was always curious. He loved learning. Whenever I could, I'd take the kids to different places on the weekend so they'd have different experiences and Tay loved it. One time, I took them on the bus to Chinatown and once that little man hopped on, he climbed and crawled all over the bus, looking out the window, wanting to see everything.

When we got to Chinatown, Tay rocked up onto his knees and pointed out the window. "Ma, there go Jackie Chan!" he shouted. "That's Jackie Chan! There are a lot of Jackie Chans."

He was so excited and I was so embarrassed. His brother and sister laughed so hard that they couldn't stop and everyone on the bus just looked at us sideways. I just got us all off the bus as fast as I could. At first, I wanted to beat Tay's ass for showing out like that, but he hadn't really done anything wrong. He didn't know and was just so excited because he loved those Jackie Chan movies. So to him, everyone of Chinese descent was Jackie Chan.

Maybe he loved those Jackie Chan movies because of all of the action that was in every scene. Because that was how Tay was himself—always active. His kindergarten teacher, Mrs. Davis, said that Tay never sat down, he was always running around; it didn't matter if playtime was over. He didn't want to take his seat.

But my son was smart. He could do everything the teacher asked him to do: write his name, recite his numbers, and he knew all the colors. That may have been the problem; he was so smart and not challenged in class because he was always disruptive.

Letters, notes or phone calls came from the school literally every other day. Getting older didn't change anything with Tay—the 1st, 2nd, and 3rd grade was all the same. The teachers told me Tay was smart, but he was disruptive, he wouldn't sit down, he wouldn't be quiet.

I was having so many problems with Tay at school that I didn't think it could get any worse, but it did. When Tay was in the fourth grade the fighting began and if I thought I'd been at the school a lot before, now it was on a whole different level. My life that became nothing but parent-teacher conferences and dealing with Tay's suspensions that seemed to come every few weeks. I stayed up at Guggenheim and now I knew how my mother felt when I was acting up like this in school. I was so tired of it, but I didn't know what to do with my son.

Tay wasn't just acting out in the classroom. This lil man used to come home with all of these different bikes. It was crazy and the conversations with him were even crazier:

I would say, "Tay, where did you get that bike?"

"My friend let me keep it.

"But, Tay, you already have a bike."

"I know, but I like his better than mine."

One day, though, a man came knocking on my door telling me that Tay had stolen his son's bike.

I was outdone, but I told the man that when Tay got home, I'd take care of it. "What does the bike look like?" I asked him.

"It's yellow and black with stunt nuts on it."

"Okay, leave me your number and I'll give you mine. And I'll give you a call once Tay gets home."

When that guy walked away from my door, and I closed the door, I was so mad. There was no need for Tay to be stealing stuff. I went to the back of the house to search for the bike, but there wasn't anything on the back porch. When I didn't find anything, I wondered if the man had made a mistake, but then, something told me to go look in the basement. And sure enough, when I walked down those steps, there was that yellow and black bike just as the man had described it.

Less than an hour after he'd left my house, I called the guy back and told him to come pick up the bike. Then, I waited for Tay to get home. I was steaming and the moment he walked in the door, I asked, "Did you take some kid's bike?"

He looked me straight in the eyes. "Nah, Ma."

"Well some kid's father came here and said you did."

"I didn't do it," he said with a straight face.

I couldn't believe he was lying straight to my face. "Keep your hands off other people's shit," I told him. "Somebody will hurt you over that."

He just shrugged, told me again again that he didn't do it and then, he walked away.

I never told him that I'd found the bike and he never said anything about the bike that he'd stolen being missing. What I did do was lock the basement, though. He wouldn't be bringing no more stolen goods up in my house.

If he wasn't stealing something from a kid, he was selling something. Just about anything that I bought for him, he'd end up selling it all—video games and other stuff...I stopped buying him anything because he wouldn't stop doing that.

But there was one bright light for Tay when he was in the fourth grade. My son was a flipper. He used to love to flip and tumble. He would flip all day, every day and that little boy could flip his ass off. He and his friends would drag these dirty mattresses that they found in the alley to the back of the house, and then, they would flip on that nasty ass mattress.

I didn't mind him flipping and tumbling, but when I saw him using those mattresses, I would beat his ass, telling him to stay off of those things where people slept and did all kinds of nasty things.

Of course, that didn't stop Tay; he was hardheaded. But then, one day all of that paid off. The Jesse White Tumblers held a session at Ada Park and they started sessions once a week.

Tay wanted to go so badly, so I paid for him to do that. Tay loved it! I was so happy that he found something that he was really interested in to occupy his time. He was so competitive, so all he wanted to do was be the best on the team. That kept him so focused.

A few months later, the team held tryouts and they wanted Tay to try out and be on that team. Tay was so excited; everyone on the team loved him and he was so talented that he made the team.

I was as excited as Tay. This would give my son something to focus on because the tumbling team traveled and performed all across the country. Tay loved being on the team, but there was a catch—the coach told Tay that he had to keep his grades up.

When his grades came out, he had two F's and the coach of the team wasn't playing. "You can continue to practice with the team, but you won't be able to perform. Not until you can bring your grades up."

Tay was devastated, but that was the end of that. He wasn't going to focus on his grades, so he had to give up the only thing that he loved at this point.

But then, I thought Tay had found a new interest when he entered the fifth grade. He joined the basketball team. Again, I was thrilled. Not only because I thought it would give him a good focus, but also because he'd be working with Coach Jones. Coach Jones and his wife (who would later become Tay's sixth grade teacher) really got involved with their students. The kids thought the coach was cool, even though he knew how to keep them in line. He put in time with the students, trying to teach them the difference between right and wrong and how going the right way was important in life. He was trying to teach the children how to make good decisions.

His wife, Mrs. Jones was the same way. She took time with her students, giving them the resources they needed not just for school, but for life.

Tay loved both of the Joneses, but even their attention to him wasn't enough. My son's attention span was off the meter. If the teacher didn't grab his attention right away, that was it—he would be off doing something else.

The only thing that worked was that Tay did love basketball and he knew if he wanted to stay on the team, like on the flipping team, he had to keep his grades up. So, he did work at that for a little while, but there was another challenge—Tay didn't like going to school. His attendance record was awful.

Once I would leave for work, Tay would come up with all kinds of lies to tell my mom and Dell about why he had to stay home from school. They would let him skip school if he had a good excuse, but before I got home from work, he'd be outside doing his thing. The only way I found out that he had missed school was because Dell would tell me. It seemed like it was every damn day when I would come home, Tay had skipped school, and then I had to go outside and find him.

Things seemed to calm down a bit when Tay got into the 7th grade. I didn't know why, exactly, but he would come straight home from school and sit under the dining room table. I guess that was the quietest place in the house for him. It was then, that he began writing. I wasn't sure what he was writing, but then, one day when I came home from work, he came from under the table.

Tay said, "Ma, listen to this."

I was tired as shit, but he got my attention. "Wait...are you doing your homework?"

"Nah, this is a rap."

"Oh, okay." So I sat down and listened, not expecting too much, but when Tay finished with this song, I was amazed. It was really, really good.

It seemed that my son had found a new interest and it changed his life. No longer did I have to go into the streets looking for him. He came home every day because he was really into his writing. I was so happy, he was focused. My hope was that some of that focus was being used for his schoolwork. Whenever I asked him about school or his homework, he told me that everything was fine. He was handling it.

Since I wasn't being called up to the school every damn day anymore, I believed him. I didn't find out the truth until I went for the regularly scheduled parent-teacher conferences and I discovered that not much had changed. Tay's teacher told me that he was still skipping school, and when he wasn't absent, he was always late, he wasn't doing is class assignments or his homework and that he would be failing if he didn't improve.

I apologized to his teacher. "It's my fault," I said. "He will do better."

I had no idea why I had taken Tay's word that he was doing his schoolwork, but when I got home, I told him about what happened to me in the fifth grade. "If you fail the eighth grade, you will have to repeat it. If you don't get your grades up, that's what's going to happen. Your friends will be going to high school, but you won't be going."

He shrugged as if what I had just said didn't bother him at all. "I don't care. I'm going to be a rapper."

"Even as a rapper, you're going to need your education. You're going to need that to do anything unless you want to be a dummy and just let people take advantage of you."

"Okay, Ma," Tay said. He was just like Booney; he didn't want to hear my mouth. So, 'Okay, Ma,' became his two favorite words.

To graduate, Tay did have to go to summer school, but at least he'd made it out of eighth grade. After graduation though, Tay was beating those streets like a wildfire, even though I told him to stay in the house until I came home from work. But he didn't listen to me. I had to come home from work and go out looking for him every damn day.

I tried to explain to him that this wasn't just about him. "When you don't come home from school, you worry your granny and Dell 'cause they don't know where you are or what happened to you. You can't keep doing that. You don't have a care in the world but other people's feelings are involved and you have to take that into consideration."

"Okay, Ma," Tay said, reciting his two favorite words.

"I'm not kidding, Tay. Your granny is too old to be worrying about where you're at or if you're okay. So stop doing that. After school, come home like you're supposed to."

"Okay, Ma."

My talk did get to Tay; he changed a little, coming straight home from school. He would sit with his granny for a little while—and then, his ass left. Before I got home, he was back out in the streets.

Tay never listened. He just did what he wanted to do. But what was interesting was that he wasn't just in the streets anymore. Now, when I asked Tay where he was, he told me he was going to the studio. He wanted to get his music made and he needed my help. Like his big brother, Tay knew my payday like clockwork and when I came home on those days, he would be there ready for me.

"Ma, I need fifty dollars for the studio."

I never had the whole $50 that he needed. After paying the bills and taking care of the kids, I was able to give him $35, $40, or $45. Every time he asked, I gave him what I could. The rest, he would get from my mom or from my niece, Iris.

As the time passed, though, I noticed that what Tay was doing was paying off. He was always well known as a kid; everybody knew him as that hardheaded, but lovable kid. But he was becoming more popular now with his music. He decided that he needed a video and I supported him with that, too. He shot his first video, *Lamron Wasted*, right at my house.

With that video, he zoomed to the top. After the popularity of that video on YouTube, he became even more focused on being a big rapper. Honestly, I couldn't figure out if I was happy for him or not because I was glad that he found something he loved and was good at, but he stayed in the streets and I feared for him. He was always in the studio, never at home anymore and when I asked where he was, he'd just say, "I'm okay, Ma. I'm at one of the guy's houses."

I never knew which guy he was talking about because he was around a lot of guys. So, all I could tell him was to be careful.

After his first video, he put out a few more. He was focused and consistent about putting his music on the Internet. Even though I was always worried about him, I had to admire how hard he was working and how committed he was. All I ever told him when we talked was, "Tay, one day it's gonna pay off."

Chapter 29

Tay was in the studio so much and working so hard that he wasn't taking care of himself. One day, he fainted and had to be taken to the E.R at Little Company of Mary Pavilion, right where I worked. When I got that call, I was so scared that I ran over to the E.R. When I got to the emergency room, Tay and his friend were just leaving and I was so happy to see that my son was all right.

"How are you?" I asked him.

"I'm fine. I just got dizzy."

"You can't keep doing what you've been doing. You've got to eat and drink plenty of water."

"I know, Ma," he said.

I wasn't slow. I knew that Tay had started smoking weed. Just like what had happened to me all those years ago, I could smell it on him. And that meant that I had to watch him even closer. "Okay," I told him. "I'll get off in a couple of hours. Make sure you come home. I wanna make sure you're fine."

"Okay, Ma."

But you know what happened. I got home, and Tay wasn't there. I texted him—no response. Then, I texted him again and again until he answered: *I'm in the studio, I'll be home as soon as I'm done, Ma.*

Of course, by the time I went to bed, he wasn't there. About two in the morning, the doorbell rang. I was half asleep when I opened the door and there was my son.

"Boy, you know that I have to get up in a couple of hours for work."

"Sorry, Ma."

I went back to bed and in a few hours when I woke up, I went into the kitchen to eat breakfast. When I opened the pantry, my mouth opened wide. The shelves were stacked with candy, potato chips, pop. There was enough stuff there to open a candy store. What the hell?

And I knew just where to go. I rushed into Tay's room and woke him up. "Where did all that shit come from in the pantry?"

Now, he was the one who was half-sleep. "I got it from a store that was going out of business."

I knew he was lying and that made me cry. He'd stolen it from somewhere. "Tay, stop bringing shit to my house." I wanted to shut that down and thought this was a good time to shut down everything. "And from now on, tell your friends to meet your somewhere else. They can't come here. I don't want none of them ringing my doorbell and none of them are allowed in my house, period!"

That was something that I had wanted to talk to Tay about for a while now. When he brought people into my house, it was never two or three friends, it was always at least double that and I hated it. I wanted all of this to stop now.

Between his not going to school, getting involved in God knows what, and spending all of his time at the studio, I worried about this kid so much and it was showing up on my body. My hair began to fall out, my blood pressure was rising and my panic attacks were getting worse, just like when I was worried about Booney. Tay's name was written over everything that was going wrong with me. I just didn't have a good feeling about his life.

I didn't want to be stressed about him because while I was worried, there were a lot of many good things happening in my son's life. Tay's career was taking off. His views on YouTube were increasing, he was becoming more popular, and he stayed really focused, shooting more videos, and making more songs. Even the people at my job knew who he was and were listening to him.

It was weird to be so worried, yet so round at the same time. I tried to talk to him, telling him all the things that my mother tried to tell me. But just like when my mom preached to me and I didn't listen, it was the same for Tay. I was living that cliché—what goes around, comes around.

Tay was just like me in that way, but not listening wasn't the only thing he got from me—Tay hated school just like I did. He went to Julian High School for maybe a week or two, but then, he had all kinds of reasons for why he didn't want to go, but what he told me the most was, "The bus ride is too long."

So, I transferred him to Robeson, but even though that was closer, that wasn't much better. There were different kids there, different gangs. And that meant there were more problems. Tay got into it with some kids at that school.

He stayed there, though. But he wasn't focused on his classes, he wasn't focused on his grades. Just like at the other schools, his teachers began to call, letting me know that he was missing classes, wasn't turning in his assignments, he just wasn't doing what he was supposed to be doing.

I didn't understand how he could get up every morning, go to school, but when he got there, he didn't perform, didn't do what he was supposed to do. But while I was asking myself those questions about Tay, I could imagine how my mother had asked those same questions about me.

Whenever I questioned Tay about school, he would just shrug and say, "I go to school every day."

"Yeah, but what do you do when you get there?" I asked him. "Are you turning in your assignments? Are you going to all of your classes? If you're not doing that, what's the point in going?"

Again, Tay just shrugged.

"Be careful," I told him. "You don't want to get kicked out of school; I told you already how important this is. You've got to get your education."

But like when my mother talked to me about it, with Tay as far as school was concerned, my words went into one ear and out the other.

❧

My son had so many new friends that I didn't know, kids who weren't from this neighborhood and that concerned me when I didn't recognize any of their faces. But these were friends that he was meeting through school and the places where he hung out.

Tay's schedule of staying at the studio continued. He was making more music, making more videos. And the more videos he put up, the more popular he became. But the more popular he became, the more problems that came. He was putting up 'diss songs' something that I had never heard of, and didn't understand until my daughter, Tania explained it to me.

"Ma, listen to Tay's music and see who he's really talking about."

But I didn't really come to understand how bad this music was until one day, I was at a grocery store and a couple of boys, about eighteen years old, approached me.

"Yo, you know him?" one of them asking, pointing to me.

I frowned. "Who?"

He pointed to my T-shirt and I had to look down to see what he was talking about. Tay had given me a shirt with the title of one of his songs: *Dis Ain't What You Want.* Then, one of the guy's said my son's name.

I shook my head. "No, this is my daughter's shirt," I said, knowing that this was nothing but trouble.

The guy growled. "You need to go take that bullshit off."

I was scared as shit. My mouth was so dry, I could hardly talk.

Even though I was carrying, (I usually carried) and I was ready for whatever was going to go down, I did exactly what that guy told me to do. I went straight home and took of that shirt, feeling for a moment like I was disowning my own son. When I saw Booney and Tay, I told them what had gone down.

"Ma," Tay said, "you can't wear that shirt outside like that."

"Shit, I didn't know that," I said. "But what kind of bullshit is this? I can't support you the way I want to?"

"Nah, Ma. There's more to it," Tay said. "It's really a long story."

All I did was shake my head. I would have to figure that story out for myself. And when I figured it out, it wasn't nice. I realized that my son had enemies. People didn't like him for one reason or another and that made me so sad.

But one thing was for sure, I never did wear that shirt again.

Chapter 30

I began to really hate Tay's music, knowing that as he got older, it was going to be a big problem. But then, Tay came home one day, and came into the living room while I was watching TV.

"Ma, I got signed to Def Jam."

Slowly, I looked up at him. "What? Shut up! For real?"

He nodded and grinned. "Yeah, Ma."

I couldn't believe it. My eighteen-year-old son had been signed by a major label. It made sense; Tay had been working so hard and he caught the attention of No ID at Def Jam and he was willing to give my son a chance. It seemed that all of that work on his music, and videos, and writing songs, and performing, and those late nights that sometimes lasted for days—all of that paid off.

Booney worked with him on the contract; he looked over everything to make sure that his brother was taken care of and then, they went to work for Def Jam. He had to work even harder to prove himself to the label, but working hard came easy to my son. He loved it.

Now, Tay had more money than he knew what to do with it. He bought clothes, shoes, jewelry and a car. He was shopping so much, I told him to be careful.

"Don't spend it all in one place. Put some away for a rainy day."

"Okay, Ma."

The only thing that wasn't good about this time was that now, Tay would leave the house and I wouldn't see him for days, then weeks and months. Not only did I miss him, but I worried about him.

But this was part of his job now, though. He had to travel from place to place, city to city to perform. But I told Tay as long as he and Booney called me and checked in regularly, that would hold me over to the next time I saw them.

They both agreed to call me regularly, but of course, neither one of my sons held their word. I used to blow their phones up when I hadn't heard from them for a few days, and they always got back to me when I did that.

It wasn't that they weren't thinking about me; my sons were just busy. They were looking out for me, though. Tay kept my rent paid and he bought me a new car. But the big thing was that Booney and Tay wanted me to quit my job.

"You don't have to work anymore, Ma."

"I want to keep working, or I'll go crazy." I had been at my job for about four years now and I really did love my job.

"No you won't. You'll find things to do, just quit, Ma."

Tay went on and on about it. "Okay, Tay," I said, though just like my son, I was going to do what I wanted to do. I planned to keep working.

Tay called me at work and told me that he was having a big video shoot on Halsted.

"Where?" I said. When he told me the shoot would be at 7220, I said, "Granny is going to kill you."

"No, she's not," he said. "There's not that many people. I posted on social media that I'm having a video shoot, but with it being in the middle of the afternoon, there won't be too many people."

If he posted it on social media....

Then, he said, "And French is doing the video with me."

For a moment, I forgot what I'd been thinking about all the people who were going to be there. "Oh, wow, French?"

"Yeah," he said.

"Okay, as soon as I get off work, I'm coming straight over there." I wanted to meet French Montana. Tay was a fan of French and he reached out to French. It was exciting that French had agreed to be part of the video.

I only had to work a few more hours, but when I got off and got over to Halsted, I couldn't believe it. Tay had said that there were only going to be a few people, but the block was filled with hundreds of people. Most of the faces I didn't recognize, but then when I saw one of Tay's old teachers, I laughed. I guess everyone had heard about this. I couldn't even get through my own street. Hell, I didn't know how I was going to get to my front door.

But I pressed through the crowd and made it to the porch. From there, I watched the entire video being made. It was so exciting. They tried to hurry through the video, knowing that surely the police would be coming soon with so many people piled in one place. But it became impossible because once French came out, the crowd went crazy. They were all trying to get into the video.

By the time police arrived, the video was over, but the people still wouldn't clear the streets. The police came in there talking shit which was the worst thing they could do. The people talked back and it went back and forth like that for a while. It took at least two hours for the police to get that street cleared. But overall the day was fun. It seemed like my son really was on his way.

Chapter 31

One morning, while I was still in bed, I got a phone call. "Ma." I could tell something was wrong by the way Booney sounded. "Tay is locked up.

"Where is he?" I asked as I jumped out of bed and got dressed while I was still talking to Booney. I was so scared and nervous. When Booney told me where he was, I rushed down to the police station.

"What's his bond?" I asked Booney.

"He doesn't have one."

"What? Why not?"

"It's a gun charge. He's being charged with gun possession."

I was shocked and appalled. I couldn't believe this. What was Tay doing with a gun and now, he was locked up with no bond? I cried and cried and cried. My son was just getting started and now this? What would happen with that now? What would happen to him?

My baby went from the county jail to prison. He was sent to Vandalia Correctional Center in Vandalia, Illinois which was about four hours from Chicago. For the next three weeks, I cried, I had headaches and my anxiety returned. I was so depressed that I could barely function. All I did was go to work, then come home and worry about my son. I waited for his phone call and thank God, he called me every day or I don't know what I would've done. He was too far for me to go visit him and that worried me.

Every day he told me the same thing, "I'm good, Ma. I'm okay. Stop worrying." But then, one time he added, "I'm scared to go to sleep."

Those words made my blood pressure rise. "Oh, my God, Tay. You're scared to go to sleep? Are they trying to hurt you?"

I was shocked when Tay started cracking up. What was funny about people in the prison trying to hurt him? But then, he said, "No, Ma. I'm afraid of the spiders and the mice. I don't get any sleep because of that."

I was relieved but mad that he had scared me that way. "Really, Tay?"

"Yeah, it's nasty in here."

"Well, I guess that means you'll think twice about going back in there."

"Yeah," he said. "I've never seen spiders like this before."

We laughed about that and then we talked about everything to take both of our minds off of where he was and what was happening. I filled him in on everything that was going on at home and by the time we hung up, I felt good. But then, I was sad all over again. I cried once again, feeling like I was never going to stop. I was so upset that Tay was in prison, but then, there was this side of me that felt at least I knew where he was. It was bad for me to feel that way, but while I was sad, there was sort of a relief. I believed my son would be safe in prison for a little while.

Tay was in prison for about three months and that was the longest three months of my life. When he came home, Tay first went to get his hair cut...and then, he went straight into the studio. He got right back to work. For a while, it felt like Tay was a changed man. He worked harder than he ever had before and I figured that was because he'd lost three months and he was making up for that time.

I'd hoped that maybe he would go back to school, but that was so far from his mind. His only focus was getting that buzz back, getting his name out there, and getting that money.

It seemed as if Tay was keeping his head down, focused on work and staying away from trouble. That gave me peace, but it only lasted for a moment.

Chapter 32

I thought all of this was behind Tay, but just a few months later, he caught another case! Another gun possession charge! At this point I was so distraught, I didn't know what to do. The first time was bad enough, but here we were again and I was afraid his time would be worse.

It was then that I knew for sure that somewhere along the time I had dropped the ball with Tay. I wasn't sure when or where, but I knew part of it was because I had let Tay run free in that studio. I let him go to the studio all the time, not monitoring him enough. He was coming and going as he pleased. I thought it was okay because he was working hard, trying to become famous. But at the same time, he wasn't grown, even though he was acting that way. So now, this was where we were.

This time, he had everyone looking for him: the US Marshalls, the police. All kinds of officers would knock on our door at all times of the day and night looking for Tay.

Just like his song said, "64th and Normal is where you can find me," and sure enough that's where they got him. That's where the police came and picked him up. I guess the police were listening to his song.

Tay had to serve three more months before he was able to go to court and get a bond. Thank God, he was in the position to pay it. This time, he was able to fight the case. I couldn't believe we were going through this again, but Tay seemed cool and calm about it. His only concern was me and not wanting me to worry.

The best way he knew how to do that was to avoid me. But that didn't help at all. That made it worse for me. That's what he would do, though—Tay would avoid me until he couldn't anymore. He knew he had to tell me what was going on.

Every time Tay came around, I tried to explain to him that he wasn't helping me by keeping me in the dark. "I don't care what's going on, good or bad, you need to tell me."

Even though I made him tell me what was going on with this case, I didn't tell my mama. She always knew that something was going on, especially when Tay stopped coming by the house.

There was a different result this time. Tay fought and he won. He beat this case. He was put on one-year probation and he couldn't violate that or he would be going back to prison.

All I could do was thank God for this.

Chapter 33

I am so proud of my son. He has honestly shown himself approved. Through all of the problems and challenges, Tay worked so hard to get to this point. Now, five albums and twelve mixtapes later, he's still evolving and I am filled with so much pride for the young man that he has become. Watching him change has been amazing as he'd grown for the better. I guess all of those speeches and lectures that he never listened to before, were paying off now. He has grown to understand everything that I was telling him through the years.

"You were right, Ma," he says to me all the time.

But to me, it wasn't about who was right or wrong; it was about listening and learning and understanding and always growing.

Tay is a man now with wisdom. He's a proud father, though he has some challenges. His children are just like him and now, he'll see. But in the meantime, he has a lot to teach them, and I hope he will do a great job.

Part 4
Toota and Tania

Chapter 34

My girls are nothing like their brothers. Both of them were so easy. While my boys are out there, my daughters are very private. You may see Tania on Snapchat or Instagram, but that's about it. Toota is on Facebook, but no where else.

As proud as I am of my sons, I am equally proud of my daughters. I had a set of strong women. Toota was like a little mean lady growing up. I always tease her about that, but she was shy, quiet and very well mannered. I never had a moment of trouble out of her. I didn't have any phone calls from the teachers about her, she didn't get into fights, and her grades were good throughout elementary and high school and when she graduated with her diploma, I was so very proud of her.

She was the next to oldest and Toota played her role well. She was the big sister who always made sure that Tay and Tania were okay. That was just what she did and to this day, her uncle calls her Mama-Toota because she was the overseer when I wasn't home. Everyone said that she was like me, but if she is, I think she is a better version. She didn't have a lot of people in her circle. She had maybe two good friends, although she was best friends with her cousin, Iris. She would hang out with them or Iris sometimes, though she never did a lot of socializing. But if she did go out, I didn't have to worry about curfew; she always came home on time.

I was so happy that Toota and Iris were so close; they were like sisters, really. Iris, being a little older, was Toota's go to person for everything and what was great was that Iris was always there for her.

When Toota worked during the summer, every single pay period, she would bring food home to her sister and brother. She never missed a beat and would do everything she could to take care of me. Toota was such a responsible young person, I never had to ask her anything,

Today, Toota continues to do well. She is married, the mother of two children and she is such a good parent. She is nothing like me; she really pays a lot of attention to her kids. For her kids, she's a teacher, a great provider and a disciplinarian. She has them involved in different activities and keeps them mentally challenged.

One thing about Toota, she will always take care of herself and her family. No matter how much success her brothers have, no matter what they give to her, she will alway work and stay her own woman.

With Tania, I was able to raise my youngest with all the knowledge that I'd gained from raising her brothers. She is strong and smart and is definitely the foundation of our family.

When she was growing up, I didn't have any problems with her until about the seventh grade. That was when she showed her ass a little, but I got her to straighten up before high school.

At first, Tania went to Dunbar, and then she transferred to Robeson, which was a bad move for her—because of who her brother was. Because of Tay, there was problem after problem after problem.

So in her freshman year, she transferred to Evergreen Park and that's where she graduated. Unfortunately, because of all the chaos, Tania didn't have a chance to enjoy her high school years.

But she has come through and now, Tania is doing very well for herself. She owns a boutique, the Girls Vault, and she's continuing her education. One of the best things is that she has a relationship with God

She doesn't have any children, but right now, she says she doesn't want any. "I have enough nieces and nephews," she always says. And just like Toota, her brothers look out for her, but she is determined to have her own.

All of my children have been so special to me, but my daughters have been my rock. They've taken care of me mentally whenever I was down. They keep me grounded and make sure that I never make moves based on emotions, which is something I've done all my life. They don't allow me to think or speak out of anger. They will tell me in a minute, "Nah, Ma! You're wrong," or "Yeah, Ma! You're right."

I love these young women and what I love the most is that they grew up to be better than me. And nothing is better than that.

Part 5
My Life

Chapter 35

As I said when I started this book, I've been through so much in my life. There were so many situations that I had to overcome: deaths in my family, being unemployed, living with my mother for so long, having my heart broken, being a single parent...and depression, anxiety and loneliness. All of these things I have come through, although I do still experience bouts of depression and anxiety.

As a young parent, I used every excuse in the book not to finish school, primarily saying that I didn't have anyone to take care of my kids...I didn't have a baby sitter. Or at other times, I used the excuse that even if I could find someone to take care of my kids, I couldn't get on the bus with all of these kids to take them to the babysitter.

But my mama wasn't trying to hear any of my excuses. She always wanted the best for me so her number one thing was to tell me to get my education. "An education will help you get a nice career and then you'll be able to take care of your kids."

Whenever she said that, I gave her one of my excuses.

None of my excuses worked with my mother, though. Especially not the bus excuse. "I've seen young people get on the bus and drop off their kids to daycare, and then go to school."

My mother was right. I'd see those girls, too. Taking the bus and dropping kids off at daycare was something that so many young parents had to do. I just never had it in me.

There were times when I just thought that I was lazy. But I always knew in my heart that there was more to it than that.

The feelings I had began when I was younger, really when I was just a kid. Back then, I didn't know what to call it or what was happening to me. I was just always sad, didn't feel good about myself, found myself always crying, feeling as if I were in a dark place. I tried to hide those feelings, though. I would cry in the shower, hoping that no one would hear me or notice my sadness. Then, I would wipe my eyes and carry on as if nothing was going on with me.

Now, I know that was depression. It was something I had as a child, as a teen and it has followed me through all the days of my life. Depression was always something that overcame me and kept me in a dark place, especially once I gave birth. And when I had to face all of those deaths: two of my brothers, my grandmother and my niece and nephew—sometimes I felt as if life was too much to bear. I didn't know how to handle that.

As my children got older, there were times when the depression became worse, probably brought on by the anxiety I had about them. I worried about my boys all the time, especially with the way Tay was in and out of court. And I worried about what would happen to Booney because of his temper. Sometimes with the boys, I felt as if my world was upside down. I didn't know if I was coming or going. My heart was so hurt because I was filled with fear for what might happen to my sons.

I never did anything about my depression, though. What was I supposed to do? I didn't understand it, then. I didn't know that it was a medical condition. So, I ignored it and tried to cover up what I was feeling. I hid it from other people and I tried to even hide it from myself by pretending that I wasn't feeling bad by spending money on things.

But no matter how much I spent on clothes, cars or other materialistic things, none of that meant shit, especially when I couldn't even enjoy the things I was buying. None of those things made me feel any better; I was too sad to be in a good place. And the biggest challenge with that was because I was in a bad place, I treated people badly. I had the nastiest of attitudes and I was mean for no reason. But I know now that hurt people hurt other people. And I was hurting badly.

I think that was why at one point in my life, I even sold crack. I was in such a low place, I didn't think of the consequences. I was hurting, so I didn't think about who I could be hurting. That enterprise didn't last long, though. But because I wasn't working, I wanted to make some fast money. It wasn't hard to hook up with one of the guys in the neighborhood to buy from, and after two weeks, I was making so much money, it was unreal.

Then one day, a customer came to me wanting four bags. She was a woman I knew, one who had really looked out for my kids through the years. If she thought they were doing something they shouldn't have been doing, she stepped in. So I sold her the four bags, but not too long after that, she came back, out of breath and sweating. Her lips were white when she asked me for three more bags.

I stood there stunned, looking at this woman I'd known for so long and who had done everything to help me. "I don't have any more," was what I finally told her.

When I closed that door, I leaned against it and just cried and cried. Seeing her that way hurt me so bad. Seeing her that way and knowing I'd caused it, hurt me even more. How could I do this to someone who cared about me and my kids?

No matter how bad I felt for myself, I wasn't going to bring anyone else down like that. I was done with that shit and when she came by my place the next night, I told her that I wasn't selling anymore. Then, I told her, "You really need to stop smoking."

She shook her head. "You don't know what I've been through. I'll stop when I'm ready and right now, I'm not. Good night."

She told my ass and I wasn't even mad at her. But that ended my time trying to sell drugs and it helped me to really look in the mirror. I needed to change my thoughts, change my mindset. I had to ask God for help. He was the only one who could help me get out of the place I was in. Only God could do it—I was that miserable.

Once I made up in my mind that I wanted to battle this depression and really change my life, I began to work on myself. I worked to change my attitude and to treat people better. I worked hard to stop crying and tried to get out of the house to do things that made me feel okay—like riding my bike and going skating. I rode my bike once a week or whenever I could. I skated and fell on my ass so many times, but that was fine because I was on the road to living my life, finding my purpose and becoming well.

I must say that now I am a changed woman. I am a better person. I love myself and because I found that love, I have confidence. Today, I am a strong God-fearing woman, but I'm still human. I will curse a little bit every now and then. But I've come a long way and I'm proud of all of the strides I've made. I don't need any kind of pat on my back from anyone; everything I've done, I've done it for myself and for others straight from my heart.

❧

I think because of my depression issues, I stayed dependent on my mother for so long, for too long. I lived with her because it was so comfortable there. I felt safe and I didn't have any major responsibilities, especially not financially. The little bit of money I had, I could spend on buying clothes and shoes and other material things for the kids and me. I spent and spent, never saving any money, never doing what my mother tried to teach me to do.

But the truth was, I stayed with my mother for so long because I was a broken young woman. And because I was so broken, I didn't take care of my children very well and in a way, I was breaking them, too. I didn't take care of them the way I wanted, the way they deserved. I provided for them, making sure they had shoes, clothes, and toys. But what I did was buy things for them, I didn't teach them, and there is a big difference. It should have been easy for me to do the right thing because I had a good example—I had my mother.

From as early as I can remember, my mother was always there trying to get me to do the right thing. She was a single parent, yet she provided and taught us so that we had her footsteps to follow in. But I didn't do it. I didn't listen to her, I didn't follow in the way she'd taught me. I didn't do it the way I was supposed to.

I wish I had listened to my mother. I wish I had listened to her from the beginning, but especially after I had my first child, Booney. I wish I had gone right back to school then. It would have been easier because I only had one baby and I hadn't been been out of school for too long. But the longer I stayed out of school, the harder it was to go back. So I didn't learn that there was more to life than just shoes, clothes, jewelry and other material things.

One thing I did well was provide for my children. With my mama and Dell, we were always able to provide for my children. They had a roof over their heads and food on the table and I made sure they had enough clothes and shoes and toys and other things that they wanted. But while I provided for them, I didn't teach them and there is a big difference. It would have been so easy for me to do the right thing since I had such a good example from my mom.

Now please, don't get me wrong. I am very close with my children. We've always been close and now that they're adults, it's the same way. We talk, we laugh, we joke, we butt heads...and to this day, they still don't listen to me. But without a doubt we love each other unconditionally.

That doesn't stop me from regretting the past and knowing for a fact that I could have done better. But the thing is, I can't go back and make it up to them. All I can do is move forward and so my eyes are on being the best that I can be. I want to be the best grandmother. I will always be there for my children, but my goal is to be a good grandmother to the twenty grandchildren that I have.

Sometimes when I look back on my life, I think I was being too hard on myself because while I did bring so much of what happened to me on myself by decisions I made and never listening to my mother, some of my behavior was in response to the sexual assaults I experienced, but at the hands of men I knew.

From the moment the new minister of music came into the church, he was creepy to me: the long stares he gave me, the way he leered at me, made me afraid every time he was close to me. I never wanted to be alone with him, but I found myself exactly that way one Friday night when we all hung out at another party. The party ended after we had to leave because of a fight, but since it was early we decided to hang out and go to our favorite fast food Chinese restaurant. We hung out there for a little while and when we got ready to leave, I went outside first.

As soon as I stepped out, I heard, "Hey, Shawnda. Come here."

It was Danny and I wanted to run the other way because no matter where I saw him, he always made me feel creepy. But he was older than me and he was the musical director at my church, so when he called me over, I went to his car.

To this day, I don't like talking about this much because of the long-lasting effects I suffered afterwards. But after I walked over to his car, he started talking to me, asking me questions the way he always did. And then, while we were standing there, Danny reached out and touched me. He grabbed my butt and grinned.

I was so shocked, I didn't know what to do. I just stood there until Kris came out of the restaurant and called me over to go with them. I didn't say a word to Danny as I turned and walked away.

When I caught up with my friends, I didn't say anything to them either. But I felt horrible and so hurt. Why had Danny touched me that way? Did he think I was like that? Was it my fault? Very quickly, I determined that what Danny had done *was* my fault. I had on really short shorts that I had put on at Kris's house because I knew my mother wouldn't let me wear them outside our house. Danny grabbed me because of the way I was dressed.

After that night, my head hung even further down, my self-esteem was lower, and I cried even more. Thinking about Danny, seeing his ugly face in my mind and that smirk on his face when he touched me made me even more depressed. It took me forever to realize that what happened wasn't my fault. I was just a kid and Danny knew better. He didn't care, though, and I would bet that I wasn't the first girl that he did that to. But those feelings of loathing stayed with me for years and I realized that's what men do when they abuse girls and women—the abusers always make the victims feel like what happened was their fault.

Then, with my self esteem already so low, I came so close to being raped. I never mentioned the name of the man who attacked me, nor did I say my neighbor's name. Until I wrote this book, she was the only person to know what almost happened that day, though she never knew any of the details.

I never shared any of these incidents with anyone because I was so ashamed. And, I was scared. I did everything thing I could not to see the guy who almost raped me again. I avoided situations where I thought he might be, I would stay away from places where I knew he would go. And I hated him for that.

But there was a lesson in both of these situations for me. I learned to become more aware and conscious of the people around me. I never put anything past anyone. So if there was one thing good that could come out of these assaults, that was it I learned lessons. And eventually, I was able to lift my head and put it behind me.

❧

While I had so many tough times, the highlight of my younger years was Rambo. When he broke my heart, that only added to my depression. I should have gone after him that day in school and explained the situation. I should have told him that I wasn't talking to another guy, I wasn't talking to anyone. He should have understood that we were just doing what kids do in school—we were all just standing together, talking and laughing. I don't know why, but after I couldn't get in touch with Rambo, I just let Rambo walk away.

In a way, though, that may have been a good thing. At that age and with all of the issues I had, I wasn't ready for Rambo. I wasn't ready for anyone because I hadn't yet learned how to love myself.

So, how could I love anyone else? Any serious relationship I may have had at that time could have been destroyed by everything I was going through, especially my depression.

Rambo left Chicago and built his own life. He had kids and clearly, I had children. But even though he was my first love, that love that I had for him never went away. No matter any of the guys I talked to, Rambo was always in the back of my mind. There were times when I had to stop myself from thinking about him and say, "Get it together, Shawnda."

And I finally did. I finally got myself together and stopped thinking about the past. Turning my life around became my focus. I decided that I wanted to change, I wanted to make myself better. It began with loving myself and understanding that I was doing the best that I could and now, I needed to do better. I wanted to get my education, find a good job, move to my own place. It took me awhile, but at least I finally did get to that point.

Once I started caring and loving myself, everything changed for me. I began working again, as a medical assistant in the same pediatric office where I was ten years before. I finally moved out and lived on my own with my children. I purchased a car and started saving money. It had taken me years to find myself, but I was so proud of my accomplishments. I was willing to work and I finally worked hard for my money. I didn't rely on that fast money at all.

It was a good time in my life. I was working hard, but also spending time socializing. I talked to and found myself relating to my patients and my co-workers and one of the things that did for me was to realize how blessed I was. There were people who had worse situations than mine. I guessed I never realized what other people were going through; I was so into my own depression before. But by feeling better about myself and listening to others,

I realized how much I had in my life. I had life and love and many people didn't have that.

As I worked, I found myself going out more and more, spending time with my co-workers from time to time. And the more I did that, the happier I became. I was in a really good place.

One night when I came home from work, I was a little bored and decided to get on the computer. Everyone had been talking about Facebook and how I needed to get on social media. I hadn't done it, so that night, I made a Facebook page.

Of course, the first thing I did after I made my page was look up Rambo. I know, it was crazy. It had been how many years since I'd last seen him? And so much had happened. We were no longer teenagers, back in high school, but I couldn't explain it. He had never left my heart.

I don't know what I expected, but I found Rambo! I couldn't believe it. I clicked on his information and read all about him and then, I went to his pictures and right away, I began to smile. Rambo looked the same, maybe even better. But he had that same gorgeous smile—that smile that always made me smile.

I was nervous, but now that I found him, I had to do something. So after taking a deep breath, I inboxed him and then waited, wondering if he would message me back. I didn't have to wait very long. Within five minutes, I had a message from him.

If I thought I was smiling before, now, I had the biggest smile on my face. We talked through Facebook until he asked me for my telephone number and I was ecstatic about two things—that he asked me for his number and that he was back in Chicago. He'd been back in the city for more than ten years.

We got off of Facebook and he called me. The moment I heard his voice, it was like old times. We talked for hours, catching up on each other's life. I told him how I'd been doing, how many kids I had, and how I was working at Little Company of Mary Pavillion. And he told me how many kids he had and he was still driving trucks. I really wanted to ask him if he was seeing someone, but I was afraid to ask.

But I did have enough courage to ask him out to dinner and we agreed to go that Sunday, Father's Day. When he came by my house, we both had the biggest grins and I think we were blushing—as if we were back in high school.

Then, at the same time, we said, "You look the same!"

We went to a Chinese restaurant and stayed there talking for hours. Finally, the question that I'd been avoiding (and he was avoiding it, too) came up.

"Are you seeing someone?" I asked him.

He shook his head. "No. If I were, we wouldn't have gotten past hello on Facebook."

We both laughed and continued talking. One of the best moments for me was finally being able to explain what happened that day in school. Even though all of these years passed, I had always wanted him to know the truth.

"I guess I shouldn't have jumped to conclusions," he said, after I explained. "But that is in the past."

"Yes, and we are in the present," I said.

We talked until we finally had to leave the restaurant and when he drove me home and dropped me off, he called me an hour later. We talked for a couple of more hours, talking each other's ears off, but we both enjoyed every moment.

When I went to work the next day, I was so excited. I told all my friends that I had found and connected with my high school sweetheart. They were all happy for me and especially when I told them the whole story and how long it had been.

"This was back in high school?" they all asked.

"Yup."

I couldn't believe it either and there was no one happier than me. From there, Rambo and I fell into a comfortable rhythm. He didn't live too far from where I worked, so he would pick me up from work and we would go have dinner when he was off. When he was working, we wouldn't see each other for days at a time, but we talked on the phone constantly when he was out driving.

I hated when he was away, always missing him like crazy and Rambo felt the same way when he had to be away from me.

"I don't like it," he said. He used to enjoy the traveling, but now, he wanted to spend more time with me. So, he put in a request with his business for local work, so he wouldn't have to leave town at all. It took a few weeks, but he finally was able to get that schedule. That was it, from there, we were able to see each other every day. I never got tired of being with him. Rambo and I would do everything together: riding our bikes, going to the zoo, walking through the park—there was nothing that we didn't want to do as long as we were doing it together. One day, we'd taken a drive a bit out of Chicago to go to a restaurant and after a couple of glasses of wine, Rambo decided that he didn't want to drive home. So we got a hotel room together and after that night, we knew we were going to be together. It wasn't too long after that when Rambo asked me to marry him.

"I want to be with you, forever, Shawnda. And I promise to love you, cherish you and take care of you."

So four months after I reached out to Rambo on Facebook, we were married on October 22, 2010. No one in our families could believe it; our relationship seemed to move quick to them, but it wasn't quick to us. We had been together just about every day and I had loved this man since I was fourteen years old. Even though it took us years to find each other again, it was clear that what was meant to be, would be.

We've been married for ten years now and to this day, he still makes me smile, he still makes me blush, he still makes me feel like I'm fourteen years old. I never thought in a million years I'd be able to say this—I truly love MY husband.

❧

What I really wanted to do in this part of the book, was to show all of the progress that I've been blessed to make. Even with all that I went through—the good and the bad, and all the things that I thought was misery, I wouldn't change a thing that happened. Everything in my life was a learning experience and because of all of my lessons, I feel as if there are many out there that I can help. Men, women and young people can learn from the things that I've gone through. My hope is that by sharing my experiences, I may be able to help others to not make the same mistakes...or if they have, to know that they can write a different ending to their story. They don't have to stay down—if they can look up, they can get up, just like I did.

That is what I hope for you. I'm hoping that if you're reading this book, you received the message that you can break the chains of whatever binds you. Many of us are living under generational curses and some of us are bound by our own mistakes. Whatever is your situation, there is always room for you to be a better you as long as you want to make a change and you know your worth.

But there is one key—you must have allies in your life and you must be willing to accept their assistance. There are people who want to help you. Whether you're dealing with depression, anxiety, rape, sexual assault, suicidal thoughts, anything—tell someone so that you can get the help and support that you need. There is no reason for you to go through any of this alone.

I wish that I'd known all of this years ago. I wish I understood back when I was a kid, that I was important. If I'd known that, I would have invested in myself sooner. I would have made a change faster. If I'd known my worth, every time I felt knocked down, I would have gotten right back up and started over, no matter how long it took for me to get it right.

It was fear that often stopped me from doing that. I was afraid because if I took the time and the chance to change, what if I didn't succeed? What if things didn't go the way I hoped? But that fear was self-imposed. That fear all came from me. But over time, I was even able to overcome fear.

One of the biggest changes I made when I decided that I wanted to change my life, was that I changed my circle. It was important for me to hang around people who had the same goals. I had to step away from anyone who wasn't about anything and surround myself with people who were goal-oriented, who wanted more in life, who were heading in the same direction that I wanted to go. These people became my support system and I was able to make many changes with their help and I am so grateful.

I am a woman of God, filled with faith and courage. I am no better than anyone on earth and that's why I know that you can get out of whatever situation you're in. Whatever mistakes bind you, whatever darkness you may feel, there is a way to make it better. Just know that even in the bad parts of your life, through the good and the bad, you are becoming better. Just remember, without the trials, you wouldn't have the triumphs. I am so happy about all of it because that is what made me who I am today. There is more out there for you, and that is the greatest lesson that I learned and that I hope that I've passed on to you.

Made in the USA
Middletown, DE
14 February 2022

61110529R00119